ALLEN COUNTY PUBLIC LIBRARY

ACR
DIS

306.
Lewis
The five ke   smart
dads

KEY HABITS OF SMART DADS

A Powerful Strategy for Successful Fathering

PAUL LEWIS

FAMILY UNIVERSITY™

ZondervanPublishingHouse
Grand Rapids, Michigan

A Division of HarperCollins*Publishers*

Allen County Public Library
900 Webster Street
PO Box 2270
Fort Wayne, IN 46801-2270

The Five Key Habits of Smart Dads
Copyright © 1994, 1996 by Paul Lewis

Requests for information should be addressed to:
Zondervan Publishing House
Grand Rapids, Michigan 49530

Lewis, Paul, 1944–
    The five key habits of smart dads : a powerful strategy for successful
fathering / Paul Lewis.
        p.   cm.
    Includes bibliographical references.
    ISBN 0-310-20667-7
    1. Fatherhood. 2. Fathers. I. Title
HQ756.L483   1994
306.874'2—dc20   94-9195
                                                              CIP

All Scripture quotations, unless otherwise noted, are taken from the HOLY
BIBLE: NEW INTERNATIONAL VERSION®. Copyright © 1973, 1978, 1984 by
International Bible Society. Used by permission of Zondervan Publishing
House.

All rights reserved. No part of this publication may be reproduced, stored in
a retrieval system, or transmitted in any form or by any means—electronic,
mechanical, photocopy, recording, or any other—except for brief quotations
in printed reviews, without the prior permission of the publisher.

Published in association with Sealy M. Yates, Literary Agent,
Orange, California.

Edited by Sandy Vander Zicht and Tim McLaughlin
Cover design by Paul Lewis
Discussion guide by Lisa Guest

Printed in the United States of America

96 97 98 99 00 01 02 03 04 / ❖DH / 10 9 8 7 6 5 4 3 2 1

To Billy L. Lewis—
my father, friend,
a very wise man,
and forever my dad.

To Leslie—
my wife, lover, best friend,
and the greatest compliment
I'll ever be paid.

To Shona, Jon, Shelley, David, and Kevin—
you are the arrows in my quiver
and my sacred assignment.
I am proud of you and humbled
to be your dad.

To every father
who feels awed by his role
or unsure about what to do.
You are not alone.

CONTENTS

Acknowledgments

I am fabulously wealthy yet deeply in debt. My wealth is my friends, and I am deeply indebted to them for their help in conceiving and writing this book.

Two summers ago Tim Vandenboss at Willow Creek Community Church near Chicago invited me to return for a second summer to Camp Paradise along the Tahquamenon River in Michigan's Upper Peninsula to speak to Chicago-area fathers and sons gathered there. For lodging he provided the White House, a small cabin about a quarter mile down river. It was there, hunched over a pad of paper at the kitchen table, gazing out the windows at a quiet river flowing lazily by, that my ideas jelled and the first sketch of the "Five Key Habits of Smart Dads" wheel took shape. Later that week, a table full of fathers surrendered their recreational time in order to critique my brainstorm. To those men who were part of that moment, this is my thank-you for your helpful and enthusiastic input.

My long-time friend Sealy Yates introduced the project to Scott Bolinder and the team at Zondervan. Both Sealy and Scott knew me through *Dads Only* (now *Smart Dads*) newsletter, which I write, edit, and publish. Their excitement for bringing these thoughts into book form and their commitment through delays along the way kept the window of opportunity open. Connie Neal set aside several weeks to help shape the first draft of the manuscript. Connie, you are a pro and more! And in the final analysis, a writer is no better than the editors who help make the ideas flow and the words sparkle: Sandy Vander Zicht and Tim McLaughlin, you have my highest praise.

My pastor, Harry Kiehl, gave time on more than one occasion to comment on what I was writing. A number of fathers attending Dads University courses in Oceanside, California, and Bellevue, Washington, also offered feedback on this book's premise. Those reality checks helped.

The taskmaster who most buoyed me, though, is Leslie—my wife, lover, companion for life. Sweetheart, you have given to me the gift of fatherhood five times. Without your tireless support and savvy, what I could have written worth reading would have made a small book indeed. I am looking forward to at least another twenty-seven years of family adventures with you.

Paul Lewis
December 1993

Introduction

While I was growing up, I don't recall ever seeing my father pull another dad aside for advice about being a good father. Maybe he did so discreetly, but I didn't notice it. He seemed to fulfill the role without much day-to-day coaching. What I observed during my childhood left me with the impression that fathering skills came naturally. In my birds-and-bees conversations with my father, he took care to explain how one *becomes* a father, but he never mentioned what it took to *be* a good father.

You may wonder why men today need to learn how to father well. Haven't previous generations of fathers succeeded at it, more or less? Yet life has taught me during my nearly fifty years that good fathering is not a matter of chance.

Learning to Father

One Sunday evening I was interviewed on a radio talk show about the Dads University courses I teach. The next morning I received a call at my office. "That fathering class you spoke about last night interests me," a man said. "I have a twenty-year-old daughter, and I'm not very happy about the way this whole thing has worked out. Could a Dads University class help me?" And before I could respond, he added, "Heck, no one teaches us men how to be dads."

The intensity of his voice echoed the emotion many men feel but seldom verbalize. Where does a father go these days to learn his craft? Should a man know intuitively how to be a good father? It seems to me that, beyond the fundamentals of protecting and providing for his children, whatever natural instincts a man has about fathering are used up about the time sperm meets ovum. Fathering, like most life skills, is learned and requires discipline.

Stop Leaving It to Chance

It was over lunch in 1977 with a friend that an intriguing idea surfaced: A newsletter of insider tips on how to be a good father. Didn't men read newsletters to keep up with careers, investments, and hobbies? Why not a newsletter on fathering? In assuming one of life's greatest assignments—a role that, more than any other, shapes a man's personal legacy—it made no sense to leave the outcome to chance and simply hope things would work.

So I conceptualized, created, and began publishing *Dads Only*—a newsletter that gave busy, fast-lane dads winning advice on building healthy relationships with their children and managing family roles well. Recently retitled *Smart Dads*, the bimonthly newsletter is read by thousands of fathers across America. It is eight tightly written pages of practical tips and insights. Twice a year a "Dad Talk" audio cassette is sent with *Smart Dads*. (See the announcement at the back of this book for more information.)

Throughout the 1980s the newsletter remained an engrossing hobby for me while I continued my career as a free-lance graphic designer and writer. But as 1990 rolled around, it became clear that—as one columnist phrased it—this would be the "Decade of the Dad." So in response to growing interest, I condensed thirteen years of study and effort in fathering into a curriculum known as Dads University.

In June of 1990 a church in East Lansing, Michigan, sponsored the first Dads University half-day course: "Secrets of Fast-Track Fathering." The feedback from those ninety-six fathers confirmed that the course filled a definite need. From that beginning, Dads University has traveled from one end of the U.S. to the other, from high school cafeterias, community centers, and church social halls to university classrooms, hotels, and corporate seminar rooms.

Experience Is a Superb Teacher

I've gathered and shared many resources about fathering. I have gleaned wisdom from thousands of dads from whom I have learned much of what I write on these pages. I have gained my best experience, however, by being a father.

If you have a child out of the nest—away at college or married—I can identify with you. My oldest daughter married four years ago. She's a fourth-grade teacher helping put her husband through his second year of law school. Typical of most firstborn children, Shona was fun-loving, always tried hard to please, and made fathering seem easy.

Which is probably why Jon came into my life. From day one Jon has been an adventurer and risk-taker. On his eighteenth birthday, the only present Jon wanted was to skydive. Fiercely independent, he challenged my directives throughout most of his first eighteen years. During the toughest two or three of those years, Jon abandoned what we had taught him and turned to drug abuse and other risky behaviors before coming to his senses. Now twenty-one,

INTRODUCTION

Jon lives on his own, employed as a locksmith while completing his last year of training to become fully certified. Once that is under his belt, he intends to return to college to earn a degree, perhaps in outdoor education, for he loves individual sports like rock climbing and surfing.

If you have a young teenager in the house, I can identify with you as well. My thirteen-year-old daughter, Shelley, is in middle school. When the phone rings these days, it's usually for her. She's a conscientious student who loves gymnastics and cheerleading. Friends and artistic endeavors run a close second. With a ready laugh and the competitive spirit of her father, she frequently wins the table games played around our house.

If you have a son or daughter in elementary school, I can still identify. My third-grader David is the sensitive one, who thinks deeply, who regularly hugs my neck with no prompting, who loves babies, books, videos, roller blading, Little League baseball, and climbing most anything.

And, if you have a toddler, preschooler, or kindergartner in the house, I can *still* relate to you. Six-year-old Kevin, our youngest, has unlimited energy and curiosity, aggressively taking on life from sun-up to sundown. He's most curious when he's thinking about how mechanical things work. If there's a repair to be done, he's right there to help me, and frustrated if he can't take part. To Kevin, real work is better than play. (I can't wait until he's old enough to mow the lawn by himself.)

These are my children. Each one is a unique challenge as I try to apply the habits of a smart dad. Each child gives me the opportunity to test, apply, and revise my fathering theories. Like you, I face the difficulties of fathering every day as I try to raise my children to become responsible adults.

One thing stands out in my conversations with dads over the years: Few things are more important to fathers than to know the deep love and respect of their children. Most of us really do want to be good fathers, even if fathering is only a frustrating fight at times. We want more depth to family relationships and a deeper connection to our children. We want our children to really know us. We want to wield our "father power" well.

I believe that most men today lack a clear picture of what a good father actually is. Without some simple guidelines to help them win at being dads, they lack the confidence that breeds success. But once a man gets a picture of what it takes to be a good father, he usually chooses to try to make that picture a reality.

FIVE KEY HABITS OF SMART DADS

In this book I will give you a picture, a model, that will help you envision and remember the five key habits of a smart dad. Over the past fifteen years, I have pondered the complexities of fathering. As with most life skills, there are a handful of key ideas that, if acted upon, yield great results. My quest has been to identify those key ideas and present them to you. The ideas you will encounter on these pages are intended to help you recognize and maximize the powerful position you occupy in the lives of your children.

1

Dad, Pop, My Ol' Man, Sir
On Being a Father

Nearing the end of his life, John Kingery was alone, abandoned by a grown daughter at an Idaho racetrack. This victim of Alzheimer's disease sat in his wheelchair, clutching a teddy bear. A note was pinned to his jacket; on his cap were the words "Proud to be an American."

When the story and photo hit the papers, Nancy Kingery Myatt—another grown daughter of the old man—discovered the father she had lost. Twenty-eight years earlier he had slipped away from his first five children, divorced their mother, and remarried. But over the years Nancy's longing for him never diminished. As far as she was concerned, he never stopped being her father.

When fifty-five-year-old Nancy greeted her eighty-two-year-old dad, he didn't recognize her, didn't know who she was, couldn't recall her name. But none of this stopped her tears when she finally saw and touched her long-lost father again.

"I didn't have a dad for all those years," she said. "Now I have one. The more I see him, the more I want to see him and talk to him."

"What my ear picked up in Nancy Myatt's words," wrote columnist Ellen Goodman, "was the simple endless hunger of a child of any age for the father who disappeared."[1]

This lost-and-found father illustrates the unquenchable power of fatherhood and the undying love of children—even adult children—for their own dads. In his condition John Kingery could do nothing for his daughter. Yet precisely because of his inability to do anything, he was reduced to the single fact of being this woman's father. And to Nancy Kingery Myatt, even that little bit of him was powerfully significant.

You are a father. You may be new at it, or you may have twelve kids. You may rate your current fathering performance as excellent, ordinary, mediocre, or poor. Whatever state you're in, you are light years ahead of Mr. Kingery in your ability to respond to your children. By merely being their father, you have tremendous power in their lives. That power does not come primarily from your fathering performance; much of it is simply inherent in the role. Your choice is not whether you will have power and potency as a father—you already do. The choice is whether you will unleash that power in constructive or destructive ways.

What Your Children Want and Need Most Is You

If you listen closely to your children they will tell you what they want from you: most important, you—then your approval, your interest, concern, guidance, and love.

Magic is in the air as I walk up the steps to my home and hear my sons inside: "Daddy's home!" How can children get so excited just because you're there? We can find it hard to believe that we matter so much to our children simply by being there. It's easier for us to think that we must perform in order to earn our child's love. There's some truth there, but only a bit. What your children want most is you.

Today at Kevin's soccer game, David told me he wanted me. He didn't say it in words, but his body language spoke it loudly: He walked up to me along the sidelines and wrapped his arms around my waist and just hung on for a while. Later he wanted me to watch his daring jump high into the air from a swing. All this mattered to David simply because I'm his father—a powerful figure in his life.

In *Father Power*, authors Henry Biller and Dennis Meredith observe that

> the principal danger to fatherhood today, and to the American family for that matter, is that fathers do not have the vital sense of father power that they have had in the past. Because of a host of pressures from society, the father has lost the confidence that he is

naturally important to his children—that he has the power to affect children, guide them, help them grow. He isn't confident that fatherhood is a basic part of being masculine and a legitimate focus of his life.[2]

Your active presence in the lives of your children is enormously powerful—probably more potent than you have imagined. No matter how nurturing, skillful, and committed a mother is, she cannot give her child a father's love. Only you can fill that void in your child's heart. It takes a father (or an effective surrogate father) to love his children with a father's love.

20th Century Fathering: A Unique Set of Challenges

Fathers at the turn of the twenty-first century face a unique predicament. Record numbers of fathers have abandoned, disowned, or otherwise given up on their children. Consciously or unconsciously, many have turned their attention and energy to arenas where success is more measurable, where men can count the rewards in dollars and cents. Our society is only beginning to tally the enormous price of fatherlessness, a price still to be paid in the currency of human lives and emotional turmoil.

Though you probably are not part of the problem (you obviously want to be a better father, or you wouldn't be reading this book), at times even you harbor mixed feelings about fathering. You're not alone. A national Gallup survey reflected such mixed feelings, concluding that "seven in ten respondents agree that the most significant family problem facing America is the physical absence of the father from the home." Virtually all adults (ninety-six percent) agree that fathers need to be more involved in their children's education. Yet only about three-quarters agree that "fathers do care enough about children's feelings" and that "most fathers are doing a good job in providing for their families financially."[3]

Even if you fully commit yourself to your children, there can be a gap between what you wish you could do and what you can actually manage. "I love my three kids more than life itself," a father told me. "I have sacrificed some very important dreams so that I can have a career that allows me to provide for my children. I have overcome substantial personal problems because I am

> **Smart Idea:**
> Mail a short note to each of your children's teachers. Express your appreciation for their dedication to education, and assure them of your support at home. The five minutes this takes will create more magic than you think.

determined to keep my marriage and family together. I am doing the best I know to do, but I am often frustrated. It takes so much work to stay competitive in my field, to provide financially, to coordinate schedules, to maintain a healthy relationship with my wife—that I never seem to have enough time with my kids. It's not a matter of wasting time on personal interests. I just don't have enough time with them, and it's not a matter of choice."

I frequently ask men what their greatest fathering frustrations are. Their most common answers are variations on their lack of time:

- **Not enough time with their children.**
- **Trying to get away from their jobs so they can have time with their kids.**
- **Finding a constructive way to use the small amount of time they have with their kids.**

In a national survey a friend and I commissioned on fathering practices, we asked dads to describe their feelings about fathering in word pictures. Here are some of their answers:

"I feel like a lone lion roaring in the jungle."

"I feel like a duck out of water."

"I feel like a loved teddy bear with all the fuzz rubbed off."

"I feel like the sun on a partly cloudy day, warm and nice when it's there, but not there quite as much as my children would like."

"I feel like a Dachshund running in deep snow."

"I feel like I'm swimming against a river of things that are demanding my time, struggling to get to the island where my children are waiting."

"I feel like water in the shower, which runs hot and cold depending on who is using water in other parts of the house."

Struggling to Find the Balance

So you're not the only father who loves his children, wants to be a good father, but is frustrated. When asked if they were stressed trying to balance home and family, seventy-two percent of men in a 1989 survey answered yes, compared with only twelve percent who answered yes in 1979.[4]

Economic Pressures

Yet economic pressures mean that men will only face greater problems as work and family commitments become more complex.

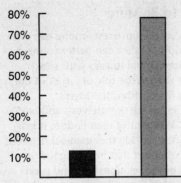

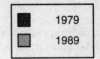

Percentage of men who answered yes to the question:
"Do you experience stress related to trying to balance work and home?"

Research shows that "since 1973, real earnings of men between 25 and 29 have declined more than twenty percent, leading some researchers to conclude that men flee family life—or are pushed out by women—because they are not reliable breadwinners."[5]

And there's the probability that serious fathering is a glass ceiling to a career—a phenomenon much discussed among women in the workplace, but now, *Time* reports, "it is the fathers who are beginning to ask themselves whether their careers will stall and their incomes stagnate, whether the glass ceiling will press down on them once they make public their commitment as parents, whether today's productivity pressures will force them to work even harder with that much less time to be with their kids."[6]

Your Fulfillment as a Father

You know the times you come home from work preoccupied or exhausted. And simply reminding yourself that the reason you go to work is to support your family doesn't automatically give you the energy to actually enjoy your time with them. You may even look for a retreat *from* your children—which is ironic, considering that they are the supposed pay-off for all your hard work. Sooner or later, every father wonders if this is all he is: Someone who works to provide for a family he doesn't have the time or energy to enjoy.

Smart Thought:
A hundred years from now the size of my bank account won't matter, nor the size or style house I lived in, nor the model car I drove. But the world may be different because I was deeply involved in the life of my children.

There Has to Be More

Recent years have witnessed a surge of interest among men to better understand who they are and how they can better connect with their children. The inadequate cultural images with which we've grown up—and which have shaped the role of father in our society—are, I believe, the driving force within the Men's Movement. It is not enough for men to see themselves—and be seen—as mere financial providers. While most men endure much emotional turmoil when they cannot provide the financial needs of their families, there is growing recognition that being a good provider isn't all a man wants out of the relationship. And it certainly isn't all his family members need from him.

If you have ever felt the indignation that says "Being a father has to include more than just providing a paycheck!" you are far more aware than society in general of who you are supposed to be as a father.

The Transformation of Fathering

How could generations of men get so far out of focus? A look at the transformation of fathering over the past two centuries can help you understand why the yearnings you feel, which tug you back to your kids, are legitimate.

In *The Third Wave* Alvin Toffler writes,

> The role system that held industrial civilization together is in crisis. This we see most dramatically in the struggle to redefine sex roles. In the Women's Movement, in the demands for the legalization of homosexuality, in the spread of unisex fashions, we see a continual blurring of traditional expectations for the sexes.[7]

Toffler maintains that the breakup of traditional roles through gender blending is one of several factors that "produce crisis in that most elemental and fragile of structures: the personality." Victims of that personality crisis, says Toffler, are anxious "to become what they are not. They work to change jobs, spouses, roles and responsibilities."

Men must resist some of the cultural changes that challenge their unique role in society. We cannot allow special-interest groups to tell us who we are, if their definition of us mars our children. I see how gender blending in our culture—as well as the demands of the Women's Movement—has confused some men about who they are and how to behave. And in their confusion, in their uncertainty about what is expected of them, they have failed to be a strong figure in their families. The result is a generation of children missing the strong paternal leadership they need.

Cultural Changes in the Role of Fathers

These powerful cultural and economic changes have us in their grip and, over the past several generations, have distanced us from our children. Yet if you understand how and why fathering has changed culturally, you can then choose whatever elements of fathering you want to reclaim as yours.

As the Industrial Revolution separated a man's home and work, fathers understandably disengaged themselves from the day-to-day routines of bringing up their children. Because their husbands relinquished these tasks, wives logically assumed them.

What emerged was what we have called "the traditional family" —Dad gone to work, and Mom keeping the home fires burning. A *Time* report states that "by the 1830s, child-rearing manuals, increasingly addressed to mothers, deplored the father's absence from the home. In 1900 one worried observer could describe 'the suburban husband and father' as 'almost entirely a Sunday institution.'"[8]

Societal Markers

If we could go back two hundred years, we would see clear social markers that defined a man's role as a father. A man in colonial America, for example, understood that he was responsible to—

- **Provide for his family's material needs.**
- **Model good citizenship by being politically informed and involved.**
- **Educate his children and teach them a trade.**
- **Understand theology and communicate absolute values to the next generation.**

Today? Fathers still feel obliged to contribute financially to the rearing of their children. They also understand that they need to contribute more than financially— but *how*, society doesn't spell out clearly. Society gives fathers mixed messages. Does

Smart Idea:
Create a "verbal sandwich" when talking with your teenager: Open with something personal, soft and gentle (the bread). Spread on some positive reinforcement (the mayonnaise). Address the problem (the lunch meat). Finish with more encouragement (another slice of bread). Tasty!

a father's masculinity bias or bless his children? Does his maleness make him less an inherent nurturer than a woman?

Fathers once gained their identity by being the sole breadwinner. But now most families depend on both mother and father to contribute financially, so a father's role as sole breadwinner is diminished. The government has also taken over the role of providing financial subsistence for low-income women and children. (It is here, in fact, that men find one of many mixed messages about their importance: one of the requirements for women to receive Aid for Dependent Children is that the father must be absent from the home. Society still recognizes the need for fathers—kind of.)

"The story we tell ourselves is a curiously old-fashioned story, that fatherhood equals economic support," contends David Blankenhorn, president of the Institute of American Values, a New York think tank that studies family issues. "But fatherhood is more than sending checks. And the consequences of fatherlessness are deep and profound and long-lasting."[9]

Beyond the duty of colonial American fathers to provide for their families' material needs, the remaining three paternal responsibilities—model informed citizenship, educate their children, and pass on absolute values—have been delegated by modern society to someone other than the father. Good citizenship and political awareness are now the domain of the public school system and the media. Education and career preparation have been turned over to public schools, colleges, and government. Theological truth is perceived by our culture as something to be kept within the church or synagogue. Whereas parents once took personal responsibility for their children's religious education, it has become the domain of the church school or other out-of-home religious institution.

Is it any wonder men in our society struggle with defining their role and measuring their success as fathers?

What Has Happened to the American Family?

"The structure of the family has been very stable over a long period of time, and it's only over the last generation that we've had this enormous change," wrote historian Christopher Lasch.[10] In a *Fortune* article entitled "The American Family, 1992," three cultural changes in the last thirty years were cited as working powerfully to restructure family life:

1. The sixties' quest for personal liberation and gratification, combined with rebellion against authority and convention, under-

mined stable family life and devalued lifelong family commitments.

2. The sexual revolution legitimized promiscuity. "The whole culture's glorification of the joy of sex without reference to marriage allowed married people to feel an unprecedented self-justification in the pursuit of sexual adventure, even if it broke up their marriages."

3. The "most vocal contingent of the Women's Movement . . . encouraged some women to see family life's inevitable constraints as an oppression from which they needed liberation. Moreover, it encouraged women to value themselves for their career achievements but not for motherhood."

The article concludes with a prescription: "Now we need to reflect on what we've learned: that children are important, that they don't grow up well unless we bring them up, that they need two parents, that our needs can't shoulder theirs aside, that commitments and responsibilities to others have to take precedence over personal gratification, that nothing is more gratifying than to see children flourish. What is our life for, if not for that?"[11]

Me-Firstism

For the last two centuries, social values have pushed a man away from putting family responsibilities first, and toward putting himself first.

"It was overwhelming," remembers a young dad about the moment he first laid eyes on his newborn. "I picked up this baby and thought, 'Here's my kid. I created him. But the money I'm going to spend on him, I could have spent on a Lamborghini.'"

The experts have their own terminology for this dad's way of thinking. Blankenhorn calls it "expressive individualism," our culture's emphasis on personal fulfillment and freedom at the expense of commitment to family and community. This "me-firstism," he argues, "dovetails with today's tendency to discount the role of fathers, to turn them into superfluous check-writers."[12]

If Patriarchy Is Passé, Who Am I as a Father?

Most men I talk with genuinely want to be good fathers to their children—but

> **Smart Idea:**
> If your child is off to college or on an extended trip, send along a special pillow case on which every family member has written (with permanent markers) words of love, respect, and encouragement. It's a great refuge at the end of a lonely day.

they are less sure about how to do it. In their uncertainty, many succumb to social pressures that make patriarchy passé. Our culture frequently treats fathers with a disregard or outright disrespect (in part because so many fathers have failed to meet the needs of their children). Society tells fathers in numerous ways that we are nearly unnecessary to the well-being of our children. Why else do so many fathers disengage with such apparent ease from their children? More than ninety percent of divorced dads are not in regular contact with their children a year later. Nineteen out of twenty single-parent families are headed by women.

• **Mr. Mom.** It does not surprise me that men have reacted in various ways against this disregard. One reaction is what I call the "Mr. Mom" approach: Dad takes on domestic duties, traditionally done by women, in an attempt to find himself as a father. It is humorous in movies—but when fathers are busy trying to be assistant mothers, who provides what only fathers can give their children? Mr. Mom simply isn't the answer, contends psychologist and author Jerrold Lee Shapiro. Fathers are more than pale imitations of mothers. "If you become Mr. Mom," he writes, "the family has a mother and an assistant mother. That isn't what good fathers are doing today."[13]

Not that a father should scorn housework. There needs to be an equitable division of labor to take care of the home and your children's needs. Merely helping out in domestic duties, however, does not fulfill your role as a father.

• **Mr. Money Bags.** Neither is the "Mr. Money Bags" reaction adequate. Such fathers act on the cultural mandate that, if nothing else, they must provide for their children. They define their fatherhood primarily in financial terms. After all, isn't it their duty to provide their children with the material possessions necessary to achieve the American Dream? So they pursue careers that give their children everything they "need"—and many of those professional or executive careers are notorious for denying fathers time with their family.

"After those at the bottom of society," believes Cornell University family expert Urie Bronfenbrenner, "the second most threatened group are those at the top, those who are supposed to be the leaders of the world—the college graduates who are having children at the start of their careers."[14] These children are left with "quality time," Myron Magnet writes in *Fortune*, "which means little time, from parents, and with what Amitai Etzioni calls 'quality phone calls': 'Honey, I won't be home. I love you.' Though not neglect in intent, this can turn out to be neglect in effect."[15]

Beyond what it doesn't do for your children, putting all your energy and time into the career basket can set you up for an identity crisis if your career is derailed. In the present economic climate, it's tough just to hold your ground, not to mention to stay on top of your career. Many who make long-term commitments to their companies, thinking thereby to cement themselves into a secure career, are devastated when their companies peel them off in corporate down-sizing. Decades of hard work and sacrifice for that coveted, supposedly tenured slot in middle management goes down the drain when such men find themselves out of a job. Some men go into a tailspin in these circumstances. If their identity is largely rooted in their careers, they experience an identity crisis as well as a financial crisis. And their frustration is doubled if they've sacrificed time with their families in hopes of acquiring security for them, only to lose on both counts. They end up with neither financial security nor the depth of relationship they really want with their kids.

Just as you would diversify a financial portfolio, you must balance your life choices to provide security and satisfaction in family relationships.

• **Mr. Outta Here.** A third reaction to society's disregard of fatherhood is "Mr. Outta Here," in which a father calls the bluff of the feminist philosophy. "You don't need me? Fine! Try getting along without me altogether." Such absentee fathers have proved their point, tragically, that children can't get along just fine without them.

More proof:

- **Fatherless daughters are 111 percent more likely to have children as teenagers.**
- **Fatherless daughters are 164 percent more likely to give birth to an illegitimate child.**
- **Fatherless daughters are ninety-two percent more likely to fail in their own marriages.**
- **Fatherless men are thirty-five percent more likely to experience marital failure.**
- **Fatherless children are twice as likely to drop out of high school.**
- **Fatherless children are failing school not because they are intellectually or physically impaired, but because they are emotionally incapacitated.**

Smart Idea:
On your next family car trip, give each child a responsibility to manage— purchasing gas, cleaning the windshield, throwing out trash, directing roadside stretching games, etc. Devote thirty minutes of each hour to a good book on tape.

- In schools across the nation, principals are reporting a dramatic rise in aggressive, acting-out behavior, especially among boys who live in single-parent homes.
- Fatherless children are fifty percent more likely to have learning disabilities.
- Fatherless children are from 100 to 200 percent more likely to have emotional and behavioral problems according to The National Center on Health Statistics.
- Fatherless young adults are twice as likely to need psychological help.
- Fatherless sons are 300 percent more likely to be incarcerated in state juvenile institutions.
- Seventy percent of all young men incarcerated in the U.S. come from fatherless homes.
- Fatherless daughters are fifty-three percent more likely to get married in their teenage years.
- The most reliable predictor of crime is neither poverty nor race, but growing up fatherless.
- More than seventy percent of all juveniles in state reform institutions come from fatherless homes.

"This trend of fatherlessness," says David Blankenhorn, founder of the Institute for American Values, "is the most socially consequential family trend of our generation."[16]

Creating a New Definition of Yourself as a Father

None of these reactions—Mr. Mom, Mr. Money Bags, or Mr. Outta Here—meet the needs of children or fulfill your own inner longing to father in a satisfying way. We must create our own definition of fathering that acknowledges cultural realities yet still allows us to regain whatever ground we've lost with our children.

I had been writing my fathering newsletter (then titled *Dads Only*) for several years when I thought one day, *I wonder what the word* father *means?* Among the variety of meanings *father* has, these two definitions leaped off the dictionary page: A father is "the source" and "that from which one derives significance."

A father is certainly a child's biological source, as is the mother, the moment sperm meets ovum. If you provided the source of life for a child, you are a father. Period. You no longer have the option to be or not to be a father. The only choice you have now is how you will manage your role and responsibility to your children.

A Father Gives Significance to His Child's Life

As the second definition of *father* suggests, children acquire their sense of significance largely from how their fathers (biological or adopted) respond to them. Particularly in our culture, mothers are expected to be deeply involved in their children's lives—with the result that children grow up with the cultural message that dads are *not* as deeply involved in a child's routine day as moms are. The social message is that a father's involvement with his children is much more optional than a mother's.

Yet this damaging cultural assumption actually works *for* fathers, because when a father gets involved with his child's school functions, for example, the perceived impact is stronger. Considering the social bias against significant fathering, a father's affirming remarks to his child—"You are valuable . . . You are a worthwhile person . . . I respect and appreciate these qualities about you"—hit home with added force. I've noticed that when kids use the phrase "My dad . . ." there is often a special pride in the inflection. And the older we grow, the more we value those things our fathers taught us, even above the skills or knowledge we learned from others.

On the other hand, I have never met individuals rejected or abandoned by their fathers who did not at sometime question their own worth or significance. One way or another, they all doubt that they could be special if their own fathers didn't see them as special.

Defying the Cultural Definitions

We are fathers in a society that loves to laud the flag, motherhood, and apple pie. Our culture esteems the successful businessman, although he may be a disaster as a father. On the other end of publicity, editors write headlines about deadbeat dads and make hard copy out of fathers who abuse their children.

Few kudos, however, are handed out to men who ran businesses, yet who excelled in fathering. The dad who puts his children ahead of his job may be quietly belittled or held back on a "daddy track," while colleagues are promoted who neglect the needs of their families

Smart Idea:
Here's how to put your child in the news when she wins an honor or does something interesting. Write a brief account of the event; then take it (with photo) to the feature, sports, business, or religion editor of your community paper. Even if the event wasn't spectacular, the boost in your child's self-esteem will be.

in order to put in long hours on the job. These are tough cultural values to resist.

You and I father in a culture whose dominant paternal images moved from "Father Knows Best" to Homer Simpson and Al Bundy, from "Ozzie and Harriet" to Ozzy Osbourne. Where once "Leave it to Beaver" children revered their fathers, sit-com characters—especially those of the seventies and eighties—publicly humiliated their dads. For thirty years or so now, fathers have been regularly portrayed in much of the broadcast media as inept, stupid, bumbling, vulgar, or harmlessly irrelevant (as former vice president Dan Quayle dared to condemn in his comments about the TV single-parent Murphy Brown).

Yet about the time this decade began, fathering became a hot topic in publishing, television, and movies. Fatherhood was the June 18, 1993, *Time* cover story. Not too long ago Bill Cosby's *Fatherhood* became one of the best-selling books of all time. Bookstore shelves are laden with books on fathering and men's issues. Before and after the seventies- and eighties-era TV programs with negative father images come reruns of Bill Cosby's character Cliff Huxtable. And then there is the critically and popularly acclaimed "Home Improvement," whose nineties' dad asserts his high-horse powered masculinity while also lovingly staying involved with his children. Movies such as *Hook*, *Field of Dreams*, *Boyz N the Hood*, and *A River Runs Through It* reflect the deep father-hunger of our generation. You also see paternal sacrifice and love displayed in distinct masculine terms in *Patriot Games*, in which a father risks his life to protect his wife and daughter.

In short, the pendulum appears to be swinging back toward acceptance if not outright applause of fathers.

Even outside the entertainment industry are positive changes. The Men's Movement gives us a forum for discussing and reclaiming our lost masculine influence on our children. Robert Bly, Sam Keen, and other prominent voices exalt fathering and encourage men to embrace their responsibilities to their children. A couple decades ago fathers began returning to the delivery room to be present at, and now assist in, the birth of their children. Now ninety percent of fathers are present at the birth of their children—instead of pacing in the waiting room, as their dads did in the fifties.[17] Birth participation is significant in that it creates a strong father-child bond early on. The jury's still out, though, on whether a father's presence at birth strengthens his commitment to the fathering task throughout the child's life.

The 1990s: The Decade of the Dad

A business friend in the office next to mine brought me a *Playboy* article entitled, "The Decade of the Dad." In this social commentary, Asa Baber offered his personal reaction to the way society has dishonored fathers.

> In our culture, the father has always been seen as a dispensable item. Portrayed as either a tyrant or a wimp, prejudiced against in divorce and child-custody actions, viewed in the media as an unnecessary appendage, considered unqualified to be included in the enormous question of abortion, available to be sent to war but rarely honored or accepted in times of peace, the father in America has been toyed with and excluded, endured and banished, mocked and misinterpreted.[18]

The heart of Baber's argument is this: Your dissatisfaction with the culture's restricting the scope of your fathering can be the fire in your belly that compels you to reclaim and deepen your fathering passions.

Once we decide to reject the images of fathering handed us by our culture, we can translate our sincere intentions into actions that play out in our decisions about career, lifestyle, and scheduling. In each decision we will lose in one area to gain in another; the fact is, we live in a society that forces us to choose between career advancement and deepening relationships with our children. So we manage this daily dilemma the best we can, trying to keep a healthy balance between work and our relationships with those who motivate us to work for their well-being.

What often energizes me to choose my kids instead of my work is the fact that I get only one shot at my kids. My kids will be two years old and six and ten and twelve only once in my lifetime. If I am not there to enjoy that moment, I miss forever the opportunity of shaping a memory. Sure, it's difficult to hang on to this perspective. But when I do, it empowers me to make more balanced decisions.

Answer Cultural Myths with Truth

The truth is this:

• **You are a father if you have given life to a child or if you have**

Smart Idea:
Write a letter to your soon-to-be-born child (or create an audio cassette). Express your joy, anticipation, and hopes for the child—and your commitment to fathering. Then tuck it away in your safe-deposit box to be pulled out and read again on the child's twelfth birthday.

assumed that responsibility through remarriage or adoption. As a father, your importance lies in your role and in your responsibility to each of your children.

- As a father, you have inherent power in the lives of each of your children. Your only choice is if you will use your power for good or ill.
- You powerfully and directly impact your children whenever you are absent from loving involvement in their lives. Although a mother can care for a child's needs, a mother cannot be a father. If you are not there for your kids, they will eventually pay a heavy toll for your absence.
- By far the most valuable thing you can give your children is a loving relationship with you, their father. The material possessions you provide are of secondary importance.
- It is *never* too late to do what is right.
- You can find success and fulfillment as a father.

You can design a winning strategy for fathering, even amid current cultural influences to the contrary. This book explains one way to simplify the demands of the job; it works for me, though I am no perfect father. As you grasp the five key habits of a smart dad, you can win at fathering—and your children win as well.

2

Cruise Control
The Power of Your Habits

"Dad, you're going the wrong way," a young voice said from the back seat. Sure enough, I was headed for the school, not toward the park for the morning's soccer practice.

"You're right, David. Force of habit, I guess." I felt a little foolish as I nosed back into the driveway to turn around.

I'm sure you've experienced lapses like this hundreds of times— moments when the force of habit prompts you to do or say the wrong thing.

Habit is a powerful force—and the key to success as a father. Habits are like cruise control: When properly set for the driving conditions, habits add ease and pleasure to the trip.

Furthermore, your habits inevitably drive you to whatever life destinations for which they've been set. So to become an effective and consistent father, any life changes I make must be made at the level of my habits. In fact, if you can make habits out of the five characteristics of smart fathering I will explore in this book, you will not have to continually struggle to be a good father. It will become second nature to you, as natural as reading the newspaper in the morning or turning on the car radio as you drive to work.

Making these five fathering habits part of your life will shape a legacy worth passing on to your children and grandchildren.

Habits: Life's Shorthand

Indeed, we are creatures of habit. When we get up in the morning, how we brush our teeth, even how we dry off after a shower—these and hundreds of other routines are prompted and guided by habit. Gratefully so. Life would be considerably more difficult if we had to decide anew every day about each of those mundane duties.

We even think in patterns laid down by habit. Researchers who study artificial intelligence (for the purpose of programming computers to think like people) have noted that we use hundreds of "scripts" as a basis for thinking. These scripts are a kind of generic story line we have composed in our heads that direct us into certain behavior in a particular situation.

No longer, for example, must you consciously think about appropriate behavior when you meet a stranger in a social situation. Somewhere along the line, you've probably programmed yourself to offer a handshake, introduce yourself, and attempt at least a little conversation of mutual interest. Such routines and internal scripts leave your mind free to grapple with matters of life that require fresh thought and decisive action.

Habits by definition are repetitive and cumulative. As you carry out an action in the same way day after day, you reap the cumulative effect of that habit. Habits of exercise and habits of eating prove this point. If you top off lunch every day with ice cream, the cumulative effect will eventually register on your bathroom scale. Similarly, the sure route to permanent, long-term weight loss is changing your eating or exercise habits. Drastic measures for short periods of time produce results of about the same duration. But dramatic changes in your health and weight can be effected by adopting a few good eating and exercise habits and repeating them until you see the cumulative effect. (Researchers say that if those who regularly drink two-percent milk switch to one-percent milk, they can lose ten pounds in a year—from that single change of habit.)

So take a careful look at your fathering habits and ask yourself if you need to adjust anything at this powerful level of habit. It's critical for obtaining long-term results. Even a single, small positive change of habit will reap its cumulative effect. It is your *habitual* fathering activities that impact your children most significantly, because they play out in your relationships over the many decades of your lifetime.

Anatomy of a Habit

Because habits are so powerful and indeed tough to change, let's look deeper. Every habit has four components: *desire*, *directions*, *diligence*, and *destination*. Understanding the interplay between these can help you evaluate habits that affect your fathering and guide you in making changes.

We may be creatures of habit, but we are *not* mere creatures. We are set apart from other animals by our ability to assess our lives, estimate the results of our decisions and actions, then choose what track to follow. With diligence, we can let habit take us along the track until we reach the destination we visualized in the first place. Desire, directions, diligence, and destination interact to form habits.

1. DESIRE →   → 4. DESTINATION
       2. DIRECTIONS → 3. DILIGENCE

First, I will never form a habit unless I can connect it to something I *desire*. (This is why you fail when you try to change a habit to please someone else.) Once you have the desire, it takes accurate *directions* to lead you toward whatever *destination* you've chosen. You carry out the directions with *diligence*—sticking with them until the desired *destination* is reached.

Now, to make each step in this sequence work for us who want to become smart dads.

Desire

Desire lies at the heart of habit. Each of your habits, good and bad, satisfy some desire. Some children, for example, discover that begging usually guarantees getting what they want. (You may remember the procedure working in your favor during your own childhood.) Until their folks wise up, the tykes play out the pattern for all it's worth.

No parent teaches a child to beg, but somehow kids stumble onto the habit, probably from noticing other kids use the technique. And after some trial and error, begging can become a toddler's habit—an early way of getting what he or she desires.

Even habits we regard as bad are spawned by desire. A man begins drinking to deaden emotional pain. He probably didn't consider drinking a bad habit until the cumulative negative effects began piling

> **Smart Thought:**
> How long has it been since your child has heard you say you were wrong? That you failed? Communication is enhanced when you admit your faults and errors and seek forgiveness.

up: a DUI arrest, a lost job, a wife's ultimatum. Even then, because drinking medicates some inner pain, he will probably continue his habit until it becomes more painful to drink than not to.

Desires also reveal our ability to imagine our future, our destination. When we set our minds on a desire, we have a goal. To reach those goals, we develop habits. To achieve the goal of a college degree, for instance, you acquire and practice habits that equip you to take clear lecture notes, to pass finals, and to research, write, and turn in a paper on time.

Directions

These kinds of directions are internal road maps that guide us in making decisions. Like it or not, we live our lives by following directions (despite the fact that men are constantly chided for failing to stop and ask for them). Directions are the how-to guides we use whenever we choose to do or not do something. These directions regularly take one or more of the following forms:

• **Specific instructions about how to perform a particular task.** Just as you may get out the car manual and follow step-by-step directions for adjusting the timing, as a father you read a credible book about discipline when your children's behavior needs particular attention.

• **Regulations to follow in a particular setting.** Laws govern our fathering behavior—laws that range from the ancient Ten Commandments to your state's vehicle code about infant car seats and safety belts. Obeying these laws habitually affects your safety and your child's well-being.

• **Beliefs and values.** Your belief in the sanctity of marriage and the preservation of the family—and the values that support them—affect your commitments to your wife and children. If you value hard work, discipline, order, and cleanliness, then these values express themselves in the directions you follow and the way you work at passing these values on to your children. The values and beliefs we model inevitably play themselves out in our children's feelings and behavior.

• **Principles to apply in particular situations.** In a given situation, you honor and adhere to a set of ideas that govern the way you respond. For instance, parents who believe the axiom "Children should be seen and not heard" enforce behavior quite different from the parent or teacher who believes, to the contrary, that children should be given the same respect accorded any person.

• **Your worldview.** That model in your mind of the way life works helps you interpret life's events—and is a major element in shaping the relationship you craft with your children.

Sprint or Marathon?

Your worldview, for example, determines whether you picture fathering as a sprint or a marathon. If you think of it as a sprint, you'll give little thought to long-term conditioning. You'll prepare far differently for an eighteen-year fathering sprint than for a fathering marathon.

A sprinter knows he can push himself to the limit as needed for a short period of time and win the race. Fathering as a marathon, however, requires a vastly different approach to your role. You can't just wing it. You have to run smart, run with endurance, run for the long haul. The expectations you have of yourself and the excuses you accept from yourself are different because of how you view fathering.

As you've probably guessed, it's the marathon runner rather than the sprinter that best represents a successful father. And the five key habits of smart dads that this book explains will help develop in you a father's endurance.

Architect or Farmer?

Here's another helpful direction finder: Do you see fathering as the work of an architect or of a farmer?

• **The architect.** The architect father believes that his assignment is to shape his child into the individual he should be when he grows up. Such a father sets boundaries for what he wants his child to become, what experiences and talents he wants his child to develop, and what kind of person his child should marry. An architect father feels it is his responsibility to cut away anything that may derail his child from fulfilling the father's design. Heaven help the musically gifted son whose architect father has already designed him as a running back, or the C-minus student headed enthusiastically for cosmetology school—but whose father wants a college degree for her. Architects

Smart Idea:
If you leave in the morning before your kids are up, write your affection and good wishes on some Post-It notes. Stick 'em to their bedroom door, bathroom mirror, in their shoe—even on their sandwich in their lunch bag.

chisel, hammer, and discipline their children to conform them to the ideals their architect fathers have in mind.

You may remember the movie *Dead Poets Society*, in which a boy commits suicide—thanks to a classic architect father in action.

Architect fathering is as stark and unhealthy as it sounds—and we all lapse into it at times, usually motivated by the best of intentions. It can seem to be the easiest, most direct path to your child's success.

• **The farmer.** The man who imagines his fathering role as a farmer waters, nourishes, and tends his children as they grow. He studies them to see what is growing there, what natural bents are showing up unique to her nature. He does his best to remove weeds that steal critical nourishment. He fights off pests. And he waits patiently, knowing that you can't rush the process of raising children, who need time to mature.

A farmer father accepts his children for the individuals they are, celebrating the growth he sees. He is as enthusiastic about a son talented in writing as he is about the daughter on her way to an athletic scholarship, even if he was shaped in his youth by neither writing nor athletics. (And you know how difficult it is *not* to channel your kids into the same hobbies and jobs and GPAs that worked for you in your formative years.)

A final word about directions as an element of habit. The trouble with directions is that you may follow *bad* ones, all the time believing that you're on the road to good fathering. You'll end up, of course, at a different destination than you had intended.

Diligence

After desire and direction, diligence goes into the making of a habit. By diligence I mean your commitment to repeat the required thought or action continually until it becomes a habit.

Diligence is the hallmark of a good father, who heeds Winston Churchill's famous wartime words, "Never, never, never give up!"

Habits have the force of motion. When you are used to behaving in a certain way, even if that way no longer serves your purposes, it is easier to continue the habit than change. This is why, if you want to replace a bad habit with a good one—or even a good one with a better one—you need diligence; for without diligently repeating a new habit pattern, you cannot overcome the force of previous habits.

Those who study human behavior say that if one practices a new behavior for twenty-one days, the behavior will become a habit.

Launching a new behavior, then, takes thought and determined, diligent effort. Constantly remind yourself that you are improving yourself for the sake of your children. Once the debris of your old habits is shoveled out of the way, the road before you will smooth out. And remember that the tough initial diligence you need to *begin* a new habit is the toughest part; once your habit is formed, living this new way will be a lot easier.

Destination

Your destination as a father is the legacy you leave for your children after your lifetime. Legacies aren't built in a day, nor would you want them to be. Like a spreading oak, strong and large from steady growth year by year, your fathering legacy is built layer by layer, action by action. Your legacy is a by-product of the thousands of mundane decisions you make and habits you follow in your fathering.

Want to leave a worthwhile legacy? Then make sure your fathering habits are leading you toward, not away from, the destination you chose for yourself.

Don't berate yourself for not having given much thought to fathering habits. You are not alone. Mothers have nine months during which their habit patterns are disrupted and reformed. As they adjust to the changes in their bodies, they gradually change their lifestyles and habits in preparation for the birth of a child. Becoming a father, on the other hand, seems to happen overnight, usually before you change any of your habits. Men generally change their fathering habits as a matter of choice.

So think about them now, if you haven't before. Deliberately developing good fathering habits now ensures that you won't be disappointed later. Start by answering the following questions:

Desire	→ How badly do I want to be a good father?
Directions	→ Am I going in the right direction to reach my desired destination? If not, am I willing to change direction?
Diligence	→ Am I willing to diligently practice some new ways, according to good directions until they become habits?
Destination	→ Have I thought about my destination as a father? Are my habits currently taking me where I want to go?

Are you willing to change any fathering habits that don't check out?

Make the Power of Your Habits Work for You

Though you have the power to choose your habits, you do not have the power to choose their consequences. Consequences play out as though on cruise control. "Sow a thought, reap an action," says the maxim. "Sow an action, reap a habit. Sow a habit, reap a character. Sow a character, reap a destiny."

How you think as a father determines how you act. While reading this book, for starters, you can choose to consider new ideas about fathering—new ideas that can change your direction, your level of diligence, and your destination. It's up to only you whether your powerful habits will either work for you or against you as a dad.

Small Changes over Prolonged Time

One advantage of habits: Small changes create major impacts. Want to reshape a fathering habit? Then don't make your first change a major one. Make several smaller changes; they will do just as well to steer you in the right direction and to your desired destination. Changing your habits, even in small and simple ways, dramatically changes your relationship with your children, especially as that habit plays itself out over years. Like compounding interest on your money, small investments in fathering add up.

> **Smart Idea:**
> Ten-minute chats are a great bedtime habit. Choose the topic from an assortment you've written in a small notebook. Try some of these ideas: My latest dream, a fear I felt today, what I'll be like when I'm older, the _____ thing I did today, etc. Date your child's answers.

After begetting a child, which may be a man's choice, our only choice is what kind of father we will be. Fathering is a daily and lifelong process, not an assignment you psych yourself up for and "do" once and be done with it. There are no shortcuts or magic formulas—only solid principles you must incorporate into your thinking, actions, habits, and character. In those dedicated to good fathering, these habits take root and shape relationships with your children.

When Rayna was seven, her dad delighted her with a bouquet of wildflowers in a soda can. He noticed the effect of this small act of kindness, and so regularly picked wildflower bouquets throughout each spring and summer. Whenever Rayna found a bouquet of wildflowers in a soda can in her room, she immediately knew that her dad was thinking of her. Rayna is a grown woman now, the mother of her own two teenagers. And guess what? Her aging daddy still leaves an unexpected wildflower bouquet on her doorstep or kitchen counter. She says it's still one of the most significant ways her father shows his love for her.

A small action that became a habit acquired a potency far beyond the mere act itself.

Don't try making big changes in your fathering tomorrow or even next week. Start with small changes—like the five key habits of a smart dad, discussed in the next chapter—and maintain them over time. In this way you can reap a lifetime of rewards.

The Five Key Habits
A Fathering Model

I worked my way through college as a free-lance graphic designer, creating more book covers, corporate logos, brochures, posters, ads, and magazine page layouts than I care to remember. The projects I really loved, though, were not these flat graphics, but three-dimensional projects—those calling for a box or display.

Leslie—my wife, my best client, and my most rigorous critic—has a business in which she creates, mats, and frames under glass one-of-a-kind, personalized statements of friendship and love. She needed a point-of-sale display to test the response to these framed messages in retail book and gift stores. So, box knife in hand, I set out with a sheet of cardboard to mock up a display. The trick in creating a display is to visualize how the parts fold and where tabs are needed to tuck into slots for adequate strength and good presentation. It took three tries just to correctly cut out a single flat sheet with side panels, tabs, and a snap-on pocket for brochures. Yet once I had a good working model as a template, it was a breeze to make several tight-fitting displays of the same design.

That working model was a *paradigm*:

• A paradigm is a serviceable tool that can help you understand, visualize, and internalize what it is you want to do.

• A paradigm represents a complex set of issues in a simple way so that you can work with them.

• A paradigm pictures something for you in a way that you can remember it, and then associate that picture with truths you can apply.

• A paradigm gives you handles with which you can grasp the information, recall it to memory, and use it whenever you find the need.

A few years ago I launched a study of fathering practices in America with Chuck Aycock, another fathering activist. Our questionnaire probed fathers for how they viewed their task, how they learned what to do as fathers, how they measured success, and much more. More than two thousand in-depth questionnaires were returned by fathers reached principally through churches and religious organizations—for here, Chuck and I assumed, would be found the most conscientious and deliberate fathers.

One of the short-answer questions we asked was, "What makes a father successful?" We wanted to discover whatever key ideas American dads used as they worked to succeed at fathering. When the answers to this question were analyzed, we were surprised to discover *no statistically significant clusters*. We could only conclude that, as a group, fathers today have no *dominant* models or ideas about fathering success to guide them in their efforts. Men apparently have no broadly held understanding of what a good father does to win. The ideas expressed about fathering success were all over the map.

So I began pondering what I could do to help men formulate a useful fathering model, a model that any man could relate to, one that linked the most important ideas and critical fathering practices with something familiar to most men. This paradigm would have to showcase the key habits that lead a dad from *desire* (to be a good father), to *directions* he needs to follow with *diligence*, so that he can arrive at his desired *destination*: A positive fathering legacy for his children.

My model is an ordinary automobile wheel—not fancy, but functional. With it I can explain five foundational fathering habits that will help you visualize your role so that you can move beyond where you are to where you want to go—which, of course, is exactly what good wheels on a car do for you.

Smart Idea:
List the names of the five best dads you know. Then create an opportunity (a note, phone call, lunch together, etc.) to ask each of them these two questions: What key ideas guide you as a father? What three family activities do you most enjoy?

Fathering does not have to be a regular fight with yourself. Fathering is fundamentally a natural function—once we understand this, all we need to do is act out our role in a habitual way. Solomon, reputedly the wisest man to walk the face of the earth, understood how one's inner world shaped one's outer practice. "As a man thinks in his heart," he said, "so is he." To reshape the way you father, then, you must reshape how you perceive fathering.

An Overview of the Five Key Habits of Smart Dads

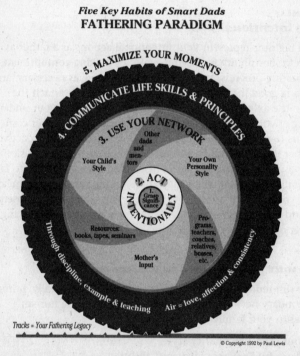

Five Key Habits of Smart Dads
FATHERING PARADIGM

5. MAXIMIZE YOUR MOMENTS

4. COMMUNICATE LIFE SKILLS & PRINCIPLES

3. USE YOUR NETWORK

2. ACT INTENTIONALLY

1. Grasp Significance

Other dads and mentors

Your Child's Style

Your Own Personality Style

Resources: books, tapes, seminars

Programs, teachers, coaches, relatives, bosses, etc.

Mother's Input

Through discipline, example & teaching

Air = love, affection & consistency

Tracks = Your Fathering Legacy

© Copyright 1992 by Paul Lewis

There is a logical, inside-to-the-outside progression in this wheel model: axle, lug nuts, rim, tire, then tread. Even the *tracks* the tread leaves have significance, for they represent the fathering legacy you leave behind for your children.

Axle:
Grasping your significance as a father

The axle on which this wheel turns represents grasping your significance as a father. Any real fathering power, any clear sense of your objectives as a dad flow from this core realization. How you habitually think about fathering and yourself as a father reflects your grasp of a father's significance. If you do not perceive the inherent, intergenerational power in your role as a dad—or if your experience with your own father has distorted your sense of a father's importance—the resulting perceptions will unhealthily mark your fathering for a lifetime and beyond. All of the other habits emanate from and turn on the axle of how you grasp your significance as a father.

Lug Nuts:
Acting intentionally

The lug nuts represent your intentional actions as a father as you take responsibility for setting goals, for making commitments, for evaluating progress, for correcting your course as necessary, and for turning good intentions into actions. As lug nuts attach the wheel to the axle, so your intentional actions connect your understanding of your fathering role to what you *do* to keep your commitments to your children. The lug nuts represent being proactive as a father instead of reactive—that is, accepting your responsibility and choosing how you will father instead of merely reacting to family and fathering crises when they arise. Acting intentionally means putting yourself in a pivotal role in the home, pursuing purposeful goals, and continually evaluating where you are as a dad, making whatever corrections you need to make along the way.

Rim:
Using your primary and secondary networks

The rim represents your fathering network—specifically, primary and secondary networks. Your primary network is the human resources in your family:

- **Your own personality style.**
- **Your child's personality and abilities.**
- **The input of your child's mother.**

Your secondary network includes—

- **Other fathers and fathering mentors.**
- **Other individuals who interact with your child, such as teachers, coaches, relatives, bosses, friends, etc.**
- **Resources that strengthen your fathering insights and skills—books, tapes, seminars, etc.**

The components of this network are available to you; you simply need to use them. In the interplay of personalities in your family and among resources outside your family, there is much strength that encourages and shapes your work as a father.

Tire:
Communicating life skills and principles

Mounted on the rim sits the tire, which represents the critical life skills and principles your child must learn from you. Between birth and the time your child leaves home, your job is to raise that child to function maturely and productively in society. Your commission is to take a helpless infant and, a few short years later, release him or her to the world—grown, prepared, and functioning as a capable adult. The steel-belted plies of the tire represent your personal example and how you apply discipline—these support the life skills and principles you work to teach your children.

And just as any tire is useless unless inflated, your love, affection, and consistency is the air, which give your fathering buoyancy and a smooth ride.

Tread:
Maximizing your moments

The tire tread in this wheel paradigm represents maximizing your moments with your child. This is the element of time. The moments you spend with your children strongly impact them for life. A loving father makes his mark on sons and daughters as he spends time in relationship with them. Different tread patterns—in our analogy, different patterns of time spent with your kids—create different effects.

The amount and quality of time you spend with your child leaves its corresponding imprint. Little or no time available to a father-child relationship is like a bald tire with dangerously little grip and faint imprint.

Tire Tracks:
The fathering legacy you leave with your child

The tracks that a tire's tread makes—memories of myriad moments spent with your child—represent the fathering legacy you leave behind. This imprint is largely shaped by the kind of life skills and

---

Smart Idea:
Take a poll tonight at dinner: "What's the most fun we've had as a family in the past month? In the past year? Ever?" Look for the reasons why and put a date on the calendar to do each again.

principles you select, and affected by whether these are communicated with love, affection, and consistency, whether you make good use of your network, whether you act intentionally, and how you grasp your own significance as a father.

(Beyond these fathering habits is the overarching issue of your worldview. As we'll explore more in chapter twelve, how you perceive the world works—that is, your life philosophy and religious views—will affect how you father. But more on this later.)

When these five habits are integrated and functioning together, you move down the road without having to think so much about the details of fathering. Good fathering will become for you a growing habit that influences your children's lives in an ongoing and cumulative manner.

To begin exploring the "fathering wheel" thoroughly, we must first consider the axle aspect: Your father's imprint on your life. Let's take a look . . .

4

Dad in the Rearview Mirror
Your Father's Imprint on Your Life

If you don't count high school, when watching my complexion and taking the zit count was a daily priority, I don't spend all that much time in front of mirrors. Approaching fifty as I am, I spend only the necessary minimum of time looking at myself—to shave, maybe blow dry and comb my hair, do a quick visual check of how my choice of attire really looks. Once in a while, though, I linger at the bathroom mirror, not checking for displaced hairs or overlooked patches of shaving cream, but studying my changing face and figure.

The other evening while channel surfing, I came across the Emmys—and there was Mr. Entertainment himself, Bob Hope. For ninety years old, Bob Hope looks great—but he *is* ninety. And even if you didn't notice that his gait is slow these days, you would detect those telltale changes in his posture, the subtle but unmistakable changes in the shape of his head and neck that come with aging.

It prompted me, an hour or so later, to linger in front of the hall mirror. Whipping around the corner, my youngest saw me just standing there. "What are you doing, Dad?"

I didn't know how to explain to him what I was doing. I don't entirely understand it myself. It's a jumble of vanity, self-talk, pity, pride, confusion, wonderment, and more than a little nonsense.

I can name one reason I mirror gaze like this: I'm assessing my father's legacy to me. There in the mirror I see my family's genetic heritage at work. When I'm in this frame of mind, after a long look in the mirror I can close my eyes and see the image of me as a young man and new dad—an image that bears a striking resemblance to the photo in our album downstairs of my father holding me, his new baby boy.

The baton is being passed. The legacy, both genetic and emotional, is being lived out.

Every father leaves a legacy. The imprint of your father is on your life, whether or not you think much about it. Your father left on you the marks of his tire tread, so to speak, whether positive or negative.

But what good does a knowledge of your father's legacy do for you? If your father was a good one, the imprint he left is a model for you to follow. In those ways that your dad was not what you wanted or needed—absent, for instance, just when you needed him most—you have a sterling opportunity to learn from his mistakes and father your children differently.

Recognizing your father's imprint on your life is the first step in grasping your own significance as a father. Understanding the natural power with which your father shaped your life will empower you to positively affect the life of your children.

Good, Bad, Indifferent

In 1992 the National Center for Fathering commissioned Gallup to conduct a national random sample of fathers across America. Among other questions, adults were asked what word best describes their relationship with their father. The resulting report, *The Role of Fathers in America: Attitudes and Behavior*, pointed out that seven out of ten described their relationship with their fathers in positive terms—"super," "great," "close," or "loving." Only seventeen percent described their relationship with their father in negative terms: "distant," "bad," or "nonexistent." Eight percent of those responding described their paternal relationship in neutral terms, such as "average" or "normal." Four percent did not answer.[1]

If you are one of the fortunate sons who could describe your relationship with your dad in positive terms, it's clear that your dad's good work as a father left on your life a positive fathering influence.

I think of when we lived in the Julian mountains behind San Diego, and of the tracks my Jeep Wagoneer left in new snow. If I were the first out on the road that morning, the perfect tracks revealed minute changes in the Wagoneer's direction, showed subtle changes in speed, and duplicated precisely the patterns of the tires' tread.

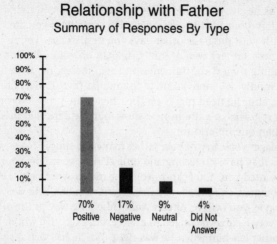

Relationship with Father
Summary of Responses By Type

70% Positive	17% Negative	9% Neutral	4% Did Not Answer

The distinct tread of an all-weather tire represents to me the influence of a father who was there for his children—an affectionate man, good role model, a man who conscientiously fulfilled his responsibilities. If this describes your father, you hardly have to think about what a good father does. You recall the moments and the feelings, and you rely on the prototype of your father.

Film actor and director Kevin Costner had this kind of relationship with his dad. In a *Parade* magazine interview, the star of *Field of Dreams* and *Dances with Wolves* says,

Cindy and I talk a lot about raising those kids. I want them to like being with their family and doing things with us, like I did with my dad—hunting, fishing together. . . . I want them to have a dad they remember. What if I'm not around when they start learning how to drive, or not home to discipline them when they come in late? Or not home for dinner with them after work, like my dad always was? I've gotta be their parent. That's the most important thing. . . . I'm not responsible for their behavior for the

Smart Tip:
Take a tip from newlyweds. Celebrate "monthiversaries" (the day of your wedding each month) with a quiet walk together . . . renewal of your wedding vows . . . a love poem from a book . . . a sexy call from the office . . . a soda with two straws. Magic!

rest of their lives, but I have to be there for them now. To tell them when they please me and why.[2]

If you are one of the seventeen percent of this country's men who, as the Gallup poll suggests, characterizes his relationship with his father as negative, I would guess you are consciously trying hard not to pattern your life like your dad's. On some days you are pleased with your progress; other days you despair that you're caught in your father's web of inflicting pain on your kids. For some fathers, calling their dads' influence on them merely negative is putting it mildly; it's more accurate to say that their fathers ran them over, and the tread marks on their hearts are proof. No pristine, solitary tracks of a tire in new snow, but the dark skid marks of more than one hit-and-run.

The images you carry of your father may have simply made you numb. You may have no feeling and little clarity about how your father imprinted you. You acknowledge the man as your father; but once you outgrew childhood, you made your own life. Your dad's fathering style, you believe, affects you neither one way or the other.

These very feelings belonged to a successful executive whom I visited. His father left him when he was eight. Yes, he has seen his dad a few times over the years, but he got the distinct impression that the relationship means little to his father. The imprint shows in the hurt he still feels from being abandoned. Yet this dad created a new pattern of fathering to overcome the pattern of abandonment his father left him with, a pattern more noticeable the more he speaks of his own children. He has aggressively poured himself into his son and daughter, taking delight in their activities and achievements.

Men floundering in deep fathering waters, with few or no models, are not alone. This decade is witnessing what may be the first generation of Americans in which a substantial number of dads have grown up without fathers in their homes. Two years after a divorce, one study shows, more than eighty percent of the noncustodial parents—generally the fathers—have little or no steady pattern of visitation with the children.

Men learn best how to be a father by watching and imitating a good one. The most important model, of course, is their own dad. Without a good dad to guide them—and no matter how strong their desire to do a better job at fathering—boys usually grow up into fatherhood with much confusion.

So whether good, bad, or indifferent, your father left his imprint on you. His presence or absence contributed to how you see yourself and how you perform a father's role. Recognizing and dealing with your father's imprint on you, particularly if it has been negative, is a prerequisite to acquiring the five key habits of smart dads.

Then, by accentuating the positive in your father's relationship with you and processing the negative, you unleash a power and freedom in you for shaping your own fresh fathering style.

The Legacy of a Bent Axle

If, as my automobile-wheel analogy suggests, the axle represents your sense of significance as a father, a destructive relationship between you and your dad is like a bent axle.

Collisions can damage axles, although you may not know it at first. The worst thing you can do is assume the axle is okay and mount a new wheel on that axle. If the axle *is* bent, the car will never drive exactly right. The wheel and tire will endure extra stress because of the distortion. The tire and any or all parts of the wheel assembly will wear out far more quickly than normal.

If you were deeply wounded in relationship with your father, you have been damaged at the core of your being. Little builds a man's sense of his significance and establishes it more deeply than to be fully accepted and loved by his own father. If your childhood relationship with your father (or a stepfather or other father figure) was bent or distorted, and you simply get on with your own fathering without recognizing and undoing the damage, you might as well mount a new tire on a bent axle.

If you still doubt that your dad could influence your own fathering as much as I claim, consider these:

• **Your father (and mother) imprinted you genetically.** Research has left no doubt that heredity shapes us. Body type, height, weight, hair color, eye color, skin color, facial features, abilities, disabilities— they are all patterned directly after the genetic code given you by your biological father and mother. Your genetic code also determines some diseases, weaknesses, and susceptibility to certain conditions, such as depression or alcoholism.

• **Your relationship with family members, including your father, teaches you how to relate to others.** In other

Smart Idea:
"Monday Night Interviews" keep kids talking. Make a 20-minute recording of their answers to your reporter-style questions about weekend activities, the day at school, pets, hobbies, friends, dreams, latest fads, etc. Send a copy to grandparents, and archive the original.

words, heredity is only part of the story. As much as genetics, how you were raised can contribute to a pattern of behavior that carries to future generations. The relationships and family interaction of your childhood created a familial pattern that, if good, you can build on; if the pattern is unhealthy, on the other hand, you need to break that pattern. Although you are not *destined* to repeat a pattern you were raised with, you are *likely* to pass on to your kids familial patterns of relating—unless you take deliberate steps to break them.

• **The relationship with your dad in particular affects how you react to your children—particularly during emotionally charged moments, when instinct takes over.** All fathers catch themselves doing, responding, or saying the very things they vowed they would never visit on their children.

Tired from an especially difficult day at the office, a dad I know of came home to the evening's first demand: a drink of water for his two-year-old daughter, who not only immediately spilled it, but fell down and hit her head, hard, on the kitchen floor. The four-year-old son, meanwhile, unaware of his sister's trauma, continued goofing around to get his father's attention. Emotionally worn before he walked in the door, standing in a puddle of water holding a toddler who was, for all he knew, seriously hurt—in the confusion and stress of the moment, he cut loose. "Stop acting like such an idiot!" he shouted at the boy—who dissolved into tears on the spot, then turned and ran to his room.

After the chaos subsided, the father reflected on his outburst. When he was a child, he remembered, his dad had routinely called him an idiot. He vowed he would never call any of his children an idiot. Yet, in a moment when his resistance was down, the words had tumbled out anyway.

• **Unhealthy ways of relating tend to be repeated in generation after generation.** The Old Testament chronicles generations of family life, and it's fascinating to see what the prophets call the "sins of the fathers" consistently appearing in the next two and three generations—even as far as the tenth generation. It is common now to discuss the persistence of generational patterns in terms of dysfunctional family systems. The "sins" of alcoholism, drug addiction, and abuse—sexual, emotional, and physical—are characteristically repeated by the victims of such behavior.

Investigate the Legacy You've Inherited

Because your relationship with your father influences how you father your children, you need to examine your legacy. Here's one way to get a handle on your fathering circumstances:

• **Complete a family genogram with as much information about your family tree as you can get your hands on.** Emotional or behavioral patterns—alcoholism, depression, abandonment, divorce, abuse, suicides, raging tempers—among your ancestors affect your life, including your fathering. The appearance of such patterns in your family tree does not mean you are destined to repeat them, but only that the odds are greater that the trait will surface, in some form, in your family. By the same token, you can trace—and reinforce—the *positive* family strengths of your ancestors, virtues that you want to preserve and pass on to your children.

FAMILY GENOGRAM

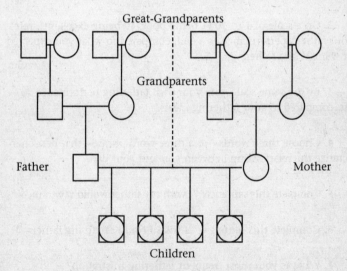

Fill in family names and shade the square or circle of any person who struggled with addiction.

• **Answer seven quick questions.** Men are generally most comfortable taking an intellectual approach to their father's impact on their lives. These seven questions may help get you out of your head and into your heart. You probably have deep feelings about your father, but you've found ways to distance yourself from your feelings. If you let yourself answer these questions honestly, you just may touch some feelings you haven't felt since childhood.

You may stir up some painful memories, but there's gold in this pain. Identifying powerful feelings from your childhood is the first step in dealing with them, which in turn can equip you with positive fathering habits for your own children.

So grab a pencil (really, get up and get one; your responses are more effective if you write them instead of merely answering in your head). Then write a brief, off-the-cuff response to the seven quick questions that follow.

Seven Quick Questions

1. How often have you and your father communicated during the last twelve months?

2. On a scale of 1 to 10 (1 being poor, 10 being excellent), rate your father's performance as a dad, compared to what you expected or wanted in a father.

3. By the same scale, rate your own fathering performance so far, compared to your fathering ideals.

4. Choose three words—or a three-word phrase—that best characterize the relationship between you and your dad.

5. Complete this sentence: "I wish my father would say to me—"

6. Complete this sentence: "I wish I could say to my father—"

7. What is your most frequent fathering frustration?

Among hundreds of confidential responses I have received to these questions, I see the following responses over and over again to the question, "Finish this statement: I wish my father would say to me—":

- You did a good job.
- You are doing well.
- Well done.
- I am proud of you.
- I respect you.
- I love you.
- I respect your life's work.
- I appreciate you.

Other responses, not so frequent, included these:

- Whatever you do, do it well. (Instead of "Do what I want you to do.")
- It's okay not to be perfect.
- Confidence counts. Don't be discouraged.
- I think these things really matter.
- I'm sorry about how things were at times.
- I wish our relationship had worked out better.
- I wish we had spent more time together.
- I want to do something with you.
- Let's try to get close.
- Let's pray together.
- I'll never drink again.
- Nothing.
- I'm back.
- I'm sorry I wasn't a good leader when you were young.
- I'm sorry for the pain.
- I don't get angry anymore.
- Let's talk.

Other men finished the statement "I wish my father would say to me—" a little differently. They talked:

- About their own problems growing up.
- About how much their parents mean to them.
- About their spiritual faith.

Clearly, father hunger is prevalent among men today. Acknowledging it is no

---

Smart Tip:
A "Saturday Box" will encourage kids to make a habit of putting things away. Agree that toys, clothes, and other items left laying around may be put in the Saturday Box— a big box in the garage or service porch—and cannot be retrieved until Saturday, no matter what. (The rule applies to you too, Dad!)

sign of weakness, either, but a positive and powerful move toward self-fulfillment and confidence in your manhood.

Alan is the eldest of three children; he has two sisters. His father was a hard-working career man in a large company. The family was well cared for, but Alan can't remember his dad ever taking much time to play ball, go fishing, or show up at his football games.

His dad helped Alan get through college, and the new graduate began a career in banking, landing eventually in mortgage lending. After fourteen years of being pushed around by corporate merger and downsizing games, Alan launched his own mortgage brokering company. It was both an economic move up and an opportunity to be his own boss.

It was on Thanksgiving that Alan's folks, now retired, visited him and his family. Sitting around the pool at the motel where his parents were staying, glass of iced tea in hand, Alan began giving his dad an update on the new business. As he talked, Alan noticed his dad nodding off—right in the middle of his son's explanations.

His dad could not have hurt Alan more if he had plunged a dagger into Alan's chest.

Over the next few months, Alan made occasional weekend trips to his parents' home in Phoenix, hoping to receive the honest expressions of approval and respect he deeply wanted from his dad. On the first two trips, the response was the same: As Alan reported the success of his business, more often than not his dad would counter by mentioning the superior successes of one of Alan's childhood friends. More and better was the inexorable quest of Alan's dad. When Alan pushed him, his dad only got frustrated. "What more do you want from me, Alan?" he said angrily. "I don't understand. I provided for you. You always had everything you needed. I got you through college. What's the problem? What do you want from me?"

On Alan's third trip home, he tried again. This time when he confronted his dad with his feelings, the dam broke, the tears and words of approval flowed, and their father-son relationship began healing.

If you uncover issues to resolve with your father, you aren't alone. To the contrary, you're in the majority. In a random survey conducted for the National Center for Fathering by the Gallup poll organization, three in five adults agreed that "most people have unresolved problems with their fathers."[3]

How to Resolve a Poor Childhood Relationship with Your Father

Once you recognize unresolved issues in your relationship with your father—issues that, in your mind, diminish your significance—you can begin to resolve them, even if your father is not available, has passed away, or is unwilling to work it out with you.

Here's how to start:

1. Recognize the Problem

It is not unusual for a child to create an idealized view of his father, especially in cases where abuse has occurred. The child learned to pretend that whatever his father requested of the child was okay; after all, to do otherwise was not allowed. Your idealized view of your father may have helped you cope as a child, but you are no longer a child. You now have the freedom and the power to be honest about your relationship with your dad.

So start by being honest about the history of events. What really happened in your relationship with your father? What are the facts? If these are not clear to you, ask your brothers or sisters or others who were there at the time to help you reconstruct what happened.

Next, be honest about your feelings. I suggest writing them out (the point of a pencil prods you to be clear and more precise than you would otherwise), putting phrases and stories down on paper so you can review your thoughts and sort out the emotions. What hurt you? What were your disappointments? What are the fears and emotional scars that remain from the hurts you received from your father? Start some sentences with "I am angry because—," "I am angry when—," "I feel angry when I recall—," and so on.

If you were forbidden in childhood to feel or express anger, it may be difficult for you to express it now. But today as an adult, if you feel angry, dare to be honest about it—and about whatever else you hold in your heart. Take time to write about any sadness or deep regrets for what did or didn't happen during your childhood.

"At first I wrote mainly about the present and the frustrations I felt with work and love," wrote Sam Osherson in his book *Finding Our Fathers*. "But then came memories and feelings about the past, about my childhood and adolescence, my

---

Smart Idea:

Take your appointment book to dinner tonight, show each family member your schedule for the next two weeks, and write in a date with each of them at the times you agree on. Then turn to the two weeks after that, and do it again.

mother and father. When my difficult and conflict-riddled relationship with my father came into focus, I realized that I had found the man I had been searching for, the father who, more by his absence than his presence, was the key to the sense of emptiness and vulnerability in my life. The journal helped me to gradually expand and enliven my relationship with my father, and to appreciate the loving and caring sides of him that had been there all along."[4]

Consider even writing a letter to your dad. Whether or not you send the letter, it's still useful to write it.

After you are honest about events and about your feelings, then talk with someone you trust—a friend who is willing to listen and affirm your right to feel whatever you may feel. (This is especially useful if your father has died, or if you cannot talk with him.)

This brings us to the next step in the process of resolving your father's impact upon you.

2. See Your Father in a New Light

• **Consider the relationship your dad had with his own father.** Your grandfather's influence on your dad had a lot to do with how well or poorly your father related to you and your siblings. How much do you know about your grandfather's performance as a dad? Find out somehow—from conversations with your grandmother, uncles or aunts, even with your father himself—about your father's history with *his* father. Any similarities between how your father was treated and how he treated *you*?

Visualizing your father as a son can help you empathize with his behavior toward you. The father of a woman I know regularly hollered and even screamed at her as a child, and seldom spoke to her in a civil tone of voice. Her father's tirades, of course, troubled her throughout childhood and adolescence.

He rarely spoke of his own father, and she never thought to ask—until after her father died, when the woman began asking relatives about her father's childhood. When she discovered that he was raised by two deaf parents, she could objectively evaluate her father's difficulty monitoring his volume. She did not excuse his verbal abuse totally, but the uncovered context helped her see her father in a more positive light.

• **Presume your father once had high hopes for you and for himself as a father.** A child naturally tends to assume—wrongly—that any deficiency in his or her relationship with a parent is the child's own fault. So try to figure out what may have disillusioned your father or dashed the hopes most dads feel. If your father withdrew or distanced himself from you, chances are that the cause was not you but pressures in his own life. Do your best to uncover what it was during your childhood that overwhelmed him or made him feel unable to be the kind of father he once hoped he could be.

• **Empathize and understand what influenced your father's behavior.** A man told me he resented the time his father had spent away from the family during a long military career. One day the adult son asked his dad why he had chosen a military career in the first place.

His dad's response was unexpected. "It was all I was sure I could do to provide for you all," he replied. He too regretted the years away from his family, he explained, but he felt that the military was the best choice, given his limited education and marketable skills.

When he put himself in his father's shoes, this son acquired an entirely new perspective of his dad. There was a connection between the two that had not been there before, for the adult son, too, was feeling the same tension between providing sufficient money for and sufficient time with his family. The son was also in a business that demanded much time away from his children, yet it provided adequate security for his family. Limited like his father in education and transferable skills, he reluctantly chose to stay in a job that kept him from his family more than he liked.

Only when he empathized with his father did this man finally recognize the tremendous love his father really had for him. For decades he had interpreted his father's absence as lack of love. Now as a man, he well understood the inner agonizing fathers endure as they are forced to choose how they will express their love for their children.

3. Presume Your Father Craved the Love and Respect of His Children

What man does not intuitively crave the love and respect of his children? Some men have disavowed this deep desire for some reason. One seventy-year-old man I know of has entirely lost contact with his children. He never speaks of them. I didn't even know he had children until a mutual friend mentioned that he had three grown children. After a brush with death, he was asked if he had contacted his children. He

Smart Idea:
Reminisce with your kids about your own childhood favorites: games, toys, teachers, playmates, foods, pets, clothes, candy, vacations, hobbies, subjects in school, adult friends, TV shows, rewards for good behavior, etc. Recall your least favorites, too.

instantly became defensive. "No, I don't care about them, and they wouldn't care about me." I don't believe a word of it. The man spent many years as an alcoholic and probably destroyed his relationship with those children. I suppose he is so certain they would reject him that he has tried to reject them first. I find it very sad to think that this man, and others may go to the grave without ever receiving the love and respect they so desperately crave.

4. You Can Give Your Father What He Will Not or Cannot Ask For

And that's forgiveness. Forgiveness cleans the slate and lets you start fresh as a father, regardless of what your father has done or failed to do for you. To forgive is to identify the wrongs done against you, recognize that they were wrong, and admit how hurt you really are.

Then you let go of what has become the burden of making your father pay for his wrongs or make it up to you. You draw a line between the past and the future; you stop using the past to excuse you from taking full responsibility for your life. Whatever the injury received from your father, you choose to leave vengeance in God's hands. A sincere apology from your dad would be wonderful—but even if your father cannot or will not see his errors or ask for your forgiveness, you can still forgive him.

And that forgiveness is your purchase order for a new axle.

His father's alcoholism ravaged his childhood, I heard a speaker recall for his audience. Before the man arrived home on payday, he had spent it all at the bar. It was no surprise when, after a childhood of shame and poverty, the son cut off all contact with his father as soon as he could. But years later someone warned him that, until he let go of the grudge he carried against his father, he would never be free. The friend suggested he recall one thing for which he could thank his father, and then express his love and gratitude for that one thing.

It took more than a few moments, but the adult son finally recalled one Christmas when his father saved enough money—he even worked a second job for a while—to buy his boy a bicycle he desperately wanted.

Later, doing his best to keep this and only this picture in his memory for at least a few minutes, the son wrote his dad a letter—not to rehearse his father's well-documented wrongs (they had covered that territory many times already), but to put aside his long list of grievances and instead express his love and appreciation for the only act of kindness he could remember from his father. He didn't know where his estranged father lived, so he mailed the letter to a relative he hoped would forward it.

It wasn't too long before the son got a phone call. His father was alone and terminally ill in the hospital—but he wanted to see his son. There at a hospital bedside, the boy received from his father the apology he had wanted, a weeping penitence for the mess the old man had made of his own life, for the wounds he had inflicted on his son. Much of what both of them had longed to say and longed to hear passed between them that day.

Shortly after that visit, the father died. His son has no regrets about his choice to forgive his dad—a choice that gave him power over his past.

Theirs was a happy ending. But there was no guarantee that the father would respond at all to his son's attempt to end the estrangement. You take similar risks when you try to resolve your relationship with your father; you know too well the hazards, perhaps, of merely communicating directly with him. So weigh the risks against the rewards before you bare your feelings to your father. If the risks seem too great to you, then wait a while until you feel comfortable to proceed.

What if you simply cannot find it in yourself to forgive your father? The freedom you will experience by forgiving him is worth seeking the professional help you may need to assist you. In any case, don't plow ahead before you take enough time to work through your own feelings first.

Most men carry inside them words they want desperately to say to their fathers, but can't for one reason or another. Men attending Dads University courses gave the following responses most often when asked to complete the sentence, "I wish I could say to my father—"

- I love you.
- I appreciate you.
- I am glad you are my dad.
- I am proud of you.
- Thanks.
- Thanks for all your work.

Other responses include these:

- I'm not always right.
- I understand how things were for you.

Smart Idea:
Preschoolers and grandkids love to wiggle through the holes you create when you lay on the floor and join your hands into a circle, raise your knees, bow your legs to join the bottoms of your feet, arch your back, etc. Add some traps and tickles.

- You've done a great job—keep it up.
- You taught me a lot.
- I wish I'd tried harder.
- I wish things could have been better between us.
- Good job, Dad. Thanks.
- Thanks for doing the best you knew how.
- What are your feelings about us, your family?
- I wish we weren't so competitive.
- Thanks for being you.
- I want to be like you, Dad.
- Thanks for having me.
- Let's pray together.
- I respect your life's work.
- I wish you had been there.
- I'm sorry.
- You need to get your life together.
- Nothing.
- I forgive you.
- Accept me for who I am.
- I need you.
- Wake up and smell the roses.
- Let's talk. I need your advice.
- I've got my own life.
- Let's go somewhere together.
- Please include me.
- Try to be a better grandparent than you were a father.

You cannot change what happened in the past, but you can go forward with your own children—beginning with your attempts to reconcile with or speak your heart to your father. You can't do anything about your ancestors, but you can do a lot about your descendants.

You can learn from your father's failures as well as from his achievements, and you can put experience, good or bad, to good use.

In our survey of fathers we asked, "What was the most significant thing your own father did with you?" We grouped the responses logically and added the headings.

The most significant thing my father did with me was—

Taught skills/values

- Taught me how to work.
- Taught me how to be honest with myself and others.

- Taught me responsibility and love.
- Taught me that the most important thing in life is one's relationship with God.

Affirmation/encouragement/support

- Supported me in activities and interests.
- He loved me and supported me in all that I did.
- Supported me in everything I did.
- Continually praised me and said how much he loved me.
- Was always available and stood by me.

Modeled a behavior/characteristic

- Set a good example.
- Set a proper example of fathering.
- Provided a model of leadership.

Shared activity

- Worked in the yard together and learned the names of plants, birds, etc.
- Spent time with me fishing and doing other things.
- Played ball with me when I was younger.
- Took time to do with me what I wanted to do.
- Spent time with me in my hobby.

Answer the question for yourself: What was the most significant thing your own father did with you? And consider how your children may one day answer this question. Their response will reflect the decisions you are making today.

A Fathering Legacy

As your father left you a legacy, you also will leave one for your children. When you recognize the imprint of your father on you, you now have a chance to choose your legacy.

Smart Idea:
Play Balloon Volleyball in the living room on a moment's notice. Lay a center line on the floor with masking tape, then two back lines—and maybe tape between two chair backs for a net. Blow up a balloon, review the rules, and play!

In one parenting program, the men are asked to write obituaries for themselves—as their children would write them.[5] This exercise cuts quickly to the bottom line—when all the fluff and glitter are stripped away, what *is* my personal bottom line? I, too, will occasionally ask a group of fathers, "What epitaph would you like to see on your tombstone?"

I hope my tombstone will read, "He was famous with his kids." What greater validation of my worth in life could there be than to have the respect of my children, who had lived with me for much of their lives and who knew me best?

It may be too late for your father to alter his legacy, but it's not too late for you. You choose and build your legacy one day at a time, one decision at a time. If you are determined to be a good dad—whether by following the good imprint your father left for you, by overcoming the negative effects of a bad relationship with your father, or by finding an effective model to follow because your father was absent—in any case, you can be a good dad.

Now for the five key habits of fathering that allow you to create the kind of legacy you want to leave for your children. It begins with another view of the axle, where fathering power begins.

Habit One:
Grasping Your Significance
The Axle

A crisp wind was at their backs, and a low afternoon sun flushed the white sails of the sloop as it heeled to starboard. Laughter and thumbs-up signals animated the interchange between six men and one thirteen-year-old son as they enjoyed an afternoon's coastal sail. No other boats were in the area, so it's anyone's guess what the boat struck. They heard a thud and felt a shudder—and then began to take on water. They came about, desperately wanting to make the distant shoreline, but it was soon apparent that they wouldn't; the boat was taking on water too fast. Their hope was reduced to life jackets and a long swim. It was every man for himself.

The boy could not keep up with the men, so his father held back to swim beside him. Up ahead in a pack, the men survived a strong current, large swells, and finally pounding surf—but each eventually dragged himself up onto the isolated beach.

Meanwhile, the boy was no match for waves, distance, and a strong undertow. Yet when his father took him in tow, he made no headway himself. At the point of exhaustion, the gut-wrenching moment came when this father realized that his boy wouldn't make it.

He could let his son drift away to his death, alone, as he swam to shore and preserved his own life. Or he could stay and die with the boy.

From the surf line, this man's anguished friends witnessed his last act on earth as he wrapped his arms around his son and stopped fighting. Several hours passed before the friends found help and could launch a search for the pair. They were never found.

Was it a father's supreme sacrifice, or did he waste his life needlessly? I don't know any more about this dad. I can't recall where I heard this story, but I've turned that father's horrendous dilemma over many times in my mind. Did he make the right decision? Was there a "right" decision? In any case, I deeply respect him for his choice. One thing is certain: This father knew how deeply significant he was to his son.

I wonder what I would do in such a crisis. Most fathers, I believe, are willing to die for their children if confronted with the stark choice. Yet we can also *live* for them as well, if we understand our enormous significance to them. Though most of us are gratefully spared the severe alternatives that the shipwrecked father had to

Five Key Habits of Smart Dads
FATHERING PARADIGM

© Copyright 1992 by Paul Lewis

choose between, we do face everyday opportunities to make tough, love-saturated, even heroic choices that balance our lives in our kids' favor.

A car axle is the point of contact between the wheel assembly and the rest of the car. Similarly, comprehending your significance as a father is what connects your fathering to the rest of your life. The axle turns the wheel, and your grasp of your own significance gives the spin to the other aspects of fathering. The fathers who literally or emotionally distance themselves from their children, who can disconnect themselves from their children, who can strand their children—these are the fathers who have no understanding of their immense significance to their children.

During his career, a friend of mine has been president of two colleges. It's demanding, high-profile work. He's good at it and he loves the profession. Yet he is as committed to his relationship with his son as he is to his innovative role in college development. More than once this busy dad shelled out $500 just to fly home in the middle of a college business trip simply to see his son play ball.

Which is all nonsense if he didn't recognize his significance as a father. But this dad knew what dividends his sacrificial expenditure of time and money would return. He acted intentionally because he knew how significant he was to his son. Because, to my knowledge, he never said, "Sorry, son—can't make it to your game this time," he strengthened the bond between him and his son.

Understanding your significance to your children routinely affects how you use time and set priorities. If you know you are significant in your child's life, for instance, you schedule time to monitor her progress. You opt to attend a conference with your child's teacher instead of deferring to her mother—even if you have to rearrange your workday to do it. If your circumstances hamper good fathering habits, you look for alternatives that instead nurture your relationship with your children. I know men who would love to take up golf, or at least lower their handicap, but they decided against it—primarily because the time it takes to get good at golf would only eat into the already-too-few hours they have to relate with their children. They aren't perfect fathers, but they know their significance to their families.

Smart Idea:
On your business card, under your occupation or title, consider adding "Father of—" followed by the names of your children. The card will launch conversations as well as make your kids feel that they get equal billing with your career.

Children Need Their Father

If your ear is tuned to it, you can hear the anguish of this generation of children. It's a cry for their fathers, a soul-deep pain that mothers, no matter how skillful or conscientious, cannot soothe. When people articulate what it was like to grow up without a father, their words pierce you.

In an essay about boyhood written for a multicultural men's studies seminar, Everett Kline, a participant in the seminar, describes the difficult adjustment of growing up without a father to guide him.

> Family was a loving mother, a gentle grandmother, a fun aunt.
> I was loved. Life was free of concerns. It was a wonderful exciting adventure.
> Then things began to change.
> When other boys began to wear long pants, I was faced with the necessity of continuing with my uncle's discards—corduroys taken in and cut-off to achieve an approximate fit and remove the worn-out knees. The teasing began; the bully had his target. How was I supposed to respond?
> New games appeared—baseball, football, basketball, hunting, fishing. How did everyone learn to play?
> What happened to the fun? I became quieter.
> Why wasn't it still enough that I had the love and softness of those central people in my life—my mother, my grandmother, my aunts—those women?
> Why wasn't I being taught how to play hard, be strong, stand up for myself, be a man? Where were the men who could teach me? They weren't there.
> Angry, confused, ashamed, I spent more time in my room tending my tropical fish. I moved, between classes, eyes averted, head bowed, my right shoulder rubbing against the wall. I wanted to disappear.[1]

Unlike Kline, fatherless boys seldom give words to their pain. They find other ways to compensate for their paternal emptiness. A Los Angeles vice chief of police ties the soaring number of kids in street gangs directly to absent fathers. "A chief characteristic of boys who join street gangs was the absence of a father," he claims. "The gangs provided a sense of protection and commitment which the absent father did not."[2]

Across town, at the Dolores Mission Church of East Los Angeles, Father Greg Boyle agrees. Once, he said, he "listed the names of the first 100 gang members that came to mind and then jotted a family history next to each. All but five were no longer living with their biological fathers—if they ever had."[3]

The Power of Your Presence Shapes Gender Identity

The mere absence of a father's physical presence can mar a child's psychosexual or gender identity. Consider the evidence:

> Early research in the area of gender-identity development focused on the effects of father absence. These early studies dealt primarily with boys, since it was believed that the detrimental influence of a fatherless home should be particularly evident in young males. Early paternal deprivation has been linked to more feminine cognitive styles, lower masculinity, higher dependence, and either less aggression or exaggerated masculine behaviors.[4]

Fatherless boys have father fantasies that are more similar to those of girls than to those of boys with fathers present. Compared to boys from intact homes, boys with fathers absent are more likely to be perceived as effeminate by social workers familiar with the boys' case histories. As adults, males from fatherless homes display less successful heterosexual adjustment than their counterparts whose fathers are present. . . .

The observable effects of paternal deprivation can take quite different forms, depending on the age at which separation occurs. Separation during preadolescence is more likely to produce exaggerated masculine behaviors than when the child is an infant or preschooler at the time of separation from the father.[5]

Researchers Shasta L. Mead and George A. Rekers scrutinized the studies on the role of the father in normal psychosexual development. This was their conclusion:

> One of the more important functions that the father fulfills in the family is to promote appropriate sex-typing in his children. The father who is either physically or psychologically absent from the home can have a detrimental effect on the psycho-sexual development of his children. On the other hand, the father who is nurturant, dominant, and actively involved in child care is most likely to have masculine sons and feminine daughters. . . .
>
> The single most important variable related to appropriate sex-role identification in children is the paternal nurturance. Consequently, the father who is affectionate toward and actively involved with his children is the father who is most likely to foster masculinity in his sons. Mussen and

Smart Idea:
Strike a deal with another couple who have kids about the same ages as yours. Once or twice a year, keep their kids for a weekend while they get away for some special time alone. They will probably be more than happy to return the favor by keeping your kids.

Rutherford (1963) found that appropriate sex-role preference in boys . . . was correlated with father-son interactions which were characterized as warm, nurturant, and affectionate. In this study, high masculinity in boys was not related to explicit encouragement for masculine behaviors from their parents or to the degree of parental masculinity or femininity. . . .

This line of research tends to support the view that boys are more likely to identify with their fathers if their interactions with them are rewarding and affectionate. Like boys, sex-role preference in girls seems to be related to a warm, nurturant relationship with the same-sexed parent, that is, the mother. However, the fathers' influence on daughters is quite different. Feminine girls tend to have highly masculine fathers who encourage feminine behaviors in their daughters.[6]

The Psychological Impact of Fatherlessness

Your presence in your child's life does more than you realize. Research has documented that children without fathers more often have the following psychological handicaps:

- **Impaired psychological differentiation**
- **Deficits in social sensitivity**
- **Deficits in social role-taking skills**
- **Increased adjustment problems**
- **A poor self-concept**
- **Low self-esteem**
- **Lowered self-confidence**
- **Less sense of mastery**
- **Less self-assertiveness**
- **Delayed emotional and social maturity and internalization of morality**
- **Higher risk for psycho-sexual development problems**[7]

While a third of children from two-parent families rank as high achievers, the percentage drops to seventeen percent from single-parent homes.[8]

You are significant to your children in dramatic ways merely by being their father and remaining committed to them. Give your child the choice between having your presence or your presents, and they'll choose *you* any day of the week.

A Positive and Continuous Relationship

Although simply being present for your children is a good start, still better is a positive and continuous relationship through which you can meet your child's psychosocial needs—needs that only you can satisfy.

Many developmental and clinical studies of children have established that, in the vast majority of cases, a father's positive presence in the home is essential for normal family strength and child adjustment—specifically, for good self-concept, higher self-esteem, higher levels of confidence in personal and social interaction, higher moral maturity, reduced rates of unwed teen pregnancy, greater internal control, and higher career aspirations.[9]

Furthermore, when it comes to cultivating a healthy sense of masculinity in a son, the frequency of interactions he has with his father matters less than the quality of the father-son relationship. Studies show that when a boy has a positive, nurturing relationship with his parents—especially with his father—the son is less likely to experience gender confusion or other psychosexual difficulties.

Finally, the degree of leadership that you assume in your family affects your child's development. Being dominant without being domineering—active participation in making family decisions, for example, and fulfilling your role as head of the home—helps your child grow into a healthy, balanced individual.

A Father Brings a Unique Strength

Your strength and role as a father is no less essential to your child's development than is the child's mother. In the *Los Angeles Times Magazine* article "Life without Father," Nina J. Easton explains how

> social thinkers across the political spectrum are beginning to emphasize the role of fathers in building safe communities. Conservative sociologist James Q. Wilson contends that while "neighborhood standards are set by mothers, they are enforced by fathers. The absence of fathers deprives the community of those little platoons that effectively control boys on the street."[10]

Fathers are enforcers of socially acceptable behavior. They set the standards for a young child, back up the mother when the child challenges her authority, and discipline the child to teach him right from wrong. When the child of an absent father reaches adolescence, the mother faces the even more demanding job of raising socially responsible children. Without

Smart Idea:
The most productive fathering time of your day may be the five minutes you stop along your route home, close your eyes, and determine your family agenda for the evening— especially your first 30 minutes.

men around as role models, adolescent boys tend to create their own dubious rites of passage and code of morals.

More Than Substitute Mothers

Some researchers buck politically correct ideology, arguing

that fathers should be more than substitute mothers, that men parent differently than women and in ways that matter enormously. They say a mother's love is unconditional, a father's love is more qualified, more tied to performance; mothers are worried about the infant's survival, fathers about future success.[11]

In other words, says David Blankenhorn,

a father produces not just children but socially viable children. Fathers, more than mothers, are haunted by the fear that their children will turn out to be bums, largely because a father understands that his child's character is, in some sense, a measure of his character as well.[12]

Jerrold Lee Shapiro, who wrote *The Measure of the Man* as well as books on fatherhood, agrees.

Mothers discipline children on a moment-by-moment basis. They have this emotional umbilical cord that lets them read the child. Fathers discipline by rules. Kids learn from their moms how to be aware of their emotional side. From dad, they learn how to live in society.[13]

As children get older, notes William Maddox, director of research and policy at the Washington-based Family Research Council, fathers become crucial in children's physical and psychological development.

Go to a park and watch a father and mother next to a child on a jungle gym. The father encourages the child to challenge himself by climbing to the top; the mother tells him to be careful. What's most important is to have the balance of encouragement along with a warning.[14]

More than common sense tells you that a child needs both parents—there's hard research, too, to support this claim:

A vast National Center for Health Statistics study found that children from single-parent homes were 100 to 200 percent more likely than children from two-parent families to have emotional and behavioral problems and about fifty percent more likely to have learning disabilities. In the nation's hospitals, over eighty percent of adolescents admitted for psychiatric reasons come from single-parent families.[15]

Dangers in Divorce

As the divorce rate started soaring a quarter century ago, so did the popular belief that divorce did not damage children *that* much. Yet recent evidence suggests that kids are not as resilient as we thought they were. A surprising 1993 article in *The Atlantic Monthly* chronicled the effect of divorce on children.

Most experts believed that divorce was like a bad cold, as far as children were concerned. There was a phase of acute discomfort, followed by a short recovery phase. According to conventional wisdom, kids would be back on their feet in no time at all.

This proved not to be the case. In 1971, when researchers conducted clinical interviews with children immediately following a divorce, they were not surprised to find that the children were traumatized. When these children were interviewed a second time one year later, however, researcher Wallerstein was surprised to discover that there had been no miraculous recovery. The children, in fact, seemed to be doing worse.[16]

When Wallerstein's findings were made public, she recalls, in came the angry letters from therapists and lawyers saying the results were undoubtedly wrong. Wallerstein's cautionary words: "Divorce is deceptive. Legally it is a single event, but psychologically it is a chain. Sometimes a never-ending chain of events, leading to relocations and radically shifting relationships."

Here are just three of her findings, which anyone with children should be aware of:

- **Five years after divorce, more than a third of children studied were experiencing moderate to severe depression.**
- **Ten years after divorce, a significant number of children studied were troubled, drifting, and underachieving.**
- **Fifteen years later, the children as adults were struggling to establish strong relationships of their own. In a word, they were relationally crippled.**

All this evidence to say that your marriage is another critical molder of your children. If you are divorced and your children seem to be handling it well, consider yourself fortunate, and redouble your efforts to mitigate the downside, even if it hasn't yet appeared. I hope your child can buck the probabilities and sail through the trauma relatively untouched.

Smart Tip:
How would you finish the sentence: "One thing my dad always said was—" How will your children finish the sentence?

Yet I must be realistic enough to say that those children are the exception. Even loving them exceptionally well as their father does not erase the emotional hit they've taken.

I don't offer this information to condemn you if you are divorced. What's done is done. Your concern now is to manage the consequences as effectively as you can and to pray for the best. If, however, you are considering divorce, don't assume that your children will work through it just fine. Do everything you can to preserve your family and protect your children from the devastating effects of divorce.

Grasping Your Personal Significance

Down at your core, at the root of your fathering habits, is your self-concept. If you have a healthy self-esteem as a *man*, you will tend to have a healthy self-esteem as a *father*. Likewise, if your masculine self-esteem is low—if you doubt yourself or believe you lack inherent value as a man—it will be difficult to see yourself positively as a father.

You aren't alone if you feel inadequate as a father or are confused about the wide range of fatherhood's requirements. And what most dads were up against, we found out from our fathering research, were things in themselves. To the question "What are the two biggest barriers you face in wanting to be a good dad?" their answers commonly included these:

- Lack of patience.
- My own imperfections.
- Feelings of inadequacy.
- Selfishness.
- Laziness.
- I don't know what I need to know about my kids at each age/stage they live through.
- I am confused over what is right.
- I have a limited education.
- I am in poor health.
- I lack experience. This leads to a lack of self-confidence.[17]

You Are Significant as You Are

Starting at your core you have the power to change so as to enhance your self-esteem and your fathering. Remember that research points out that it is your *availability to* and *love for* your children that are central to their well-being. Whatever your limitations—personal problems you need to deal with, a sinking self-esteem that needs a boost—work through them. But in the meantime, don't miss the fact that you are significant to your child, exactly as you are this moment.

You Can Change—from the Inside Out

Genuine character development always flows from the core of who you are. So whatever change you want to make as a father, begin with an inner, core change. Here's how Stephen Covey describes this kind of change in his book *The Seven Habits of Highly Effective People*:

> This new level of thinking is . . . a principle-centered, character-based, "inside-out" approach to personal and interpersonal effectiveness. "Inside-out" means to start first with self; even more fundamentally, to start with the most inside part of self—with your paradigms, your character, and your motives.
>
> It says if you want to have a happy marriage, be the kind of person who generates positive energy and sidesteps negative energy rather than empowering it. If you want to have a more pleasant, cooperative teenager, be a more understanding, empathic, consistent, loving parent. . . .
>
> The inside-out approach says that private victories precede public victories, that making and keeping promises to ourselves precedes making and keeping promises to others. It says it is futile to put personality ahead of character, to try to improve relationships with others before improving ourselves.[18]

Fathering Success Is within Your Grasp

When we asked our survey group, "What makes a father successful?" many fathers in our survey cited personal qualities.

- **Humility and patience**
- **Ability to be real, genuine, and touchable—no macho image**
- **Ability to love truthfully**
- **Willingness to give of his time and affection**
- **Being a good role model**
- **Being a good example**[19]

Smart Idea:
Take photos of your kids doing things right—daily chores, cleaning their rooms, grooming a pet, doing homework, helping mom, dad, a sibling. Set aside special pages in the family album for these snapshots.

None of these are beyond your grasp. They begin every time with a deliberate choice. Sure, consistency may take a while, but with practice the growth of these qualities in you could be dramatic. You *can* practice humility and patience. You *can* honestly love your children. You *can* be real, genuine, and touchable. You *can* give your time and affection. You *can* be a good example and role model.

Want a place to start? In particular, you can make fairly quick progress as a father by giving your child your love, your approval, and your encouragement.

Your Child Needs Your Love

In *Psychology Today's* "Who Is the New Ideal Man?" reader survey, several respondents cited their own fathers as the ideal man. I noted that it was no extraordinary quality embodied in fathers that made them ideal to their children, but rather the simple love he gave them. "My father made me feel so loved and so important," one woman wrote, "that I feel ideal enough about myself to enjoy living and growing."[20]

Your Child Needs Your Approval

Listen to the words of two men, both well-known. One received the approval of his father; the other did not.

"I guess like every kid, what I most wanted was to please. I still care a lot what people think of me," remembers actor-director Kevin Costner. "I wanted to be liked by my dad most of all. I still do.

"As a kid, when my dad was coming home, my brother and I used to wait for him. He was a working guy, a lineman for Edison, and we used to race to undo the laces of his boots. My brother'd take the left boot, and I'd take the right, just really glad my dad was there. I wanted so much to please him."[21]

Singer B. J. Thomas, best known for his 1969 hit "Raindrops Keep Fallin' on My Head" and winner of five Grammy awards, grew up lacking what he most wanted to achieve through his music. His childhood seems to him now like one long search for ways to win his father's approval. Then the boy discovered that his father liked country and western music.

"Ultimately, Dad gave me music," Thomas says. "He was probably my first motivation to be a singer, so I love him for that. It was the only way I could get him to talk to me. I learned songs by Earnest Tubbs and Hank Williams, and I'd sing my tail off to him. And he'd just cry."[22]

Although B. J. Thomas succeeded on a grand scale financially and professionally, none of it could take the place of the approval he needed from his father—approval that was nearly impossible to get.

Your child needs massive and regular expressions of approval from you. And don't cheapen it by tossing casual, generic compliments in the general direction of your child. Instead praise what you can honestly praise about your child. Don't tell her the obvious exaggeration that she is the most beautiful girl in the world. She will trust your sincerity, however, if you're more inclined to say "Wow, your hair looks pretty braided that way."

Kevin Costner received a precious gift that laid the groundwork for a positive self-worth: the approval of his father. B. J. Thomas was deprived of his father's approval and has consequently struggled his entire life with his self-esteem.

What I found interesting about these two entertainment giants was that neither of their fathers achieved anything publicly notable. No grand talents or exploits. Just ordinary men with ordinary jobs and the ordinary personal shortcomings. Although the alcoholism of B. J. Thomas's father marred the family, I wonder if his dad understood that even with his alcoholism, his son needed his approval.

It is the mark of the male parent, I think, to fix our attention on whether we deserve our children's approval, while we ought to consider *their* hunger for approval from whatever kind of fathers we are, good, bad, or ugly.

Your Children Need Your Encouragement

All children need to know that someone is out there pulling for them, that someone in the stands is cheering them on. More important, children need to know that their *fathers* are there to encourage them. Because children look first and most to their parents for that encouragement, a cheerleading father helps his son discover his competence, helps his daughter perceive her ability to be successful, useful, self-actualized.

You see this phenomenon every weekend at athletic events and school plays. When Dad is on the sidelines encouraging his child, the child plays better. When Dad is in the audience, the child performs her

Smart Idea:
Tonight at the dinner table, switch places—everyone sits in someone else's customary chair—with this assignment: During the meal, they must behave like the family member whose chair they're sitting in. If you don't die of laughter first, you'll learn a lot.

best. A child may still excel without a father there to watch her, but the achievement is not as sweet.

"Bucky" Dent appeared on "Oprah" last summer. He plays shortstop for the Yankees. Raised by an aunt, he was nonetheless led to believe that the aunt was his mother. When he finally learned who his mother was, Bucky wanted the truth from her about his father, too. But his mom clammed up—and even forbade Bucky to make contact with him.

Although this void was sorely felt by Bucky, he still imagined during boyhood games that his father was there in the stands, just like the fathers of his teammates.

Only when Bucky became an adult did his mother finally relent and tell him who his father was. It turned out that this dad knew exactly who his son was—had followed Bucky's entire athletic career, in fact. He actually *had* attended football games and *had* cheered his son on, without Bucky ever realizing it. When Bucky heard this, a great need inside him was finally fulfilled.

Never Too Late to Start

As long as your children are alive, it is never too late to start developing habits of loving, approving, and encouraging your child—never too late to start cheering.

I have talked with dads who say they have failed with their first child. They mature, have another child, do better this time—but often dismiss their responsibilities to the first child. Yet he is the only biological father that first child will ever have, even if he was a flawed father.

In the case of Baby Jessica, you may remember, two sets of parents battled each other for months to gain custody of a little girl. Dan Schmidt, the baby's birth father, also had a thirteen-year-old daughter, Amanda—but Amanda he had not claimed or supported. She watched her father, the only father she had, fight tooth and nail to claim Baby Jessica while he did nothing to claim her. Before all the world, her dad demonstrated that he valued his new family far more than he valued Amanda.

In reality, Schmidt's negligence of Amanda probably stemmed more from a poor self-perception than from outright indifference toward his daughter. Because he is her father, however, no amount of explaining diminishes the devastation Amanda experienced.

Personal Effects of Grasping Your Significance as a Father

Let's admit it—men enjoy the feeling of our own power and significance. If you derive your significance from your work and career—if it is there that you feel important and highly esteemed—you will understandably feel motivated to work hard. Working in such a situation enhances your self-image. In short, you treasure your career.

"Where your treasure is," noted Jesus Christ, "there your heart will be also." If I find my significance—my treasure—primarily in my work, that's where my attention and my time will be focused. Yet when I have grasped my significance as a father, I will treasure *that* role and opportunity increasingly.

Recognizing your significance as a father elevates and invigorates even your ordinary tasks. Instead of merely "baby-sitting" your kids when their mom is out for an evening, you'll call it what it is—fathering! One man added these words to his business card, under his name and title: "Father of Steven and Carri." Clarity about who you are is the issue here.

No Plainer Words

You are significant by virtue of being the father of your children. Your presence and your family leadership is significant. You have exclusive abilities to meet your child's needs for love, approval, and encouragement. You are a massive power in the life of your child. You are absolutely crucial to their growth, wholeness, and well-being.

If you've got hold of your significance as a father, the engine is running, the transmission is engaged, the axle is turning in the right direction—now you're ready to tackle the second key habit of a smart dad.

Smart Idea:
If a kid on your block is receiving too little parental attention, include him in one of your family activities, even if it's just a short trip to the store or the park. Make it a point to tell his parents what good characteristic you observed in their child.

6

Habit Two: Acting Intentionally

The Lug Nuts

Too bad fathering isn't organized like football—players who are highly conditioned, safely equipped, and well-trained . . . an offensive unit, a defensive unit, and special teams for kickoffs, punt returns, field goals, on-side kicks.

If fathering were like football, we'd have everything from newborn fathering specialists to crisis-control specialists for fathering teenagers. The patient dads would help with homework and building science projects, while others would specialize at discipline, reasoning with toddlers, coaching soccer teams, and paying college bills.

On the other hand, we *do* parent like football—at least, how they *originally* played football. The same eleven played offense, defense, kick-off, punt return. There were no special teams. Every player did his best in any game situation.

When it comes to raising kids, the easiest half of the game to play is defense. At least that's what many dads spend most of their time doing. We respond. We answer questions when our kids ask them, not before. We step in to referee fights or dish out discipline when they harass their mom. Otherwise, we try to be a nice guy who minds his own business.

Defensive fathering is a wonderful fantasy. But it's fuzzy thinking like this that keeps us ineffective and out of the game until we're so far behind that catching up is nearly impossible.

Intentional action is what good fathering requires—and that's what the lug nuts represent in my analogy. Lug nuts secure the wheel to the axle. In fathering, your intentional actions (lug nuts) connect your understanding of your significance as a father (axle) to the living out of that understanding in your relationship with your children (the rim, tire, etc.).

Five Key Habits of Smart Dads
FATHERING PARADIGM

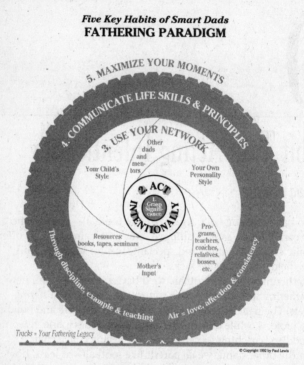

Tracks = Your Fathering Legacy

© Copyright 1992 by Paul Lewis

Two Companies

Intentional action, unfortunately, characterizes only one of the two companies in a man's life: the company he owns or works for, and the family or home company, of which he is supposedly the senior partner.

It's only reasonable to expect that, if your sense of significance comes primarily from your professional status and accomplishments, then it will be at the office where you will want to excel with goals, action plans, and other demonstrations of intentional action. Furthermore, if you do not understand your true significance at home as a father and husband, you simply won't look to home for satisfaction and payoffs. You'll charge hard all day in the workplace and arrive home tired, emotionally spent, and hoping your home and family will be a tranquilizer for you.

Now imagine this: How would you feel if, as you head out to work tomorrow morning, you knew that no one in your company had given any concrete thought to the company's mission? No written business plan, no goals, no quarterly projections, no one-year or five-year plan for growth, no one pouring over the sales figures and comparing them to projections. How secure would you feel about the future of your company and your job there?

In an economy like ours, we hear everywhere, only careful planning, review, and course corrections by corporate management keep things moving forward and profitably. *A family needs the same care and consideration as a corporation.* Aren't the dynamics of your family's security, success, and future much the same as a company's? Don't family relationships deserve some of the same definition, planning, review, and energy you give to setting and reaching your business goals? When we realize that our homes and families yield benefits so enormously more important than any amount of corporate ladder climbing can yield, we will treat our family relationships with more care and respect.

So what's stopping you from applying in your family the same intentional action you already practice at the office? Set goals, schedule production, do some evaluation and review, bring new services on line.

What Men Want at Home and Work— and What Women Want for Them

What men want in our jobs and companies is *growth*. We tend to be frustrated unless the company's going somewhere. For our families, however, we tend to value not growth, but *stability*. If I'm out slaying dragons all day in the field or the office, I don't want to walk in the front door of my home that evening to fight more dragons. I want the home front calm and stable.

Wives, to no one's surprise, often have very opposite agendas for their husbands. They want family life—the home corporation—to be a growing enterprise, where

> **Smart Idea:**
> "Dear Abby" letters in your newspaper can spawn family dialogue. Read a letter—but not the printed advice, until family members have suggested their solution. Were yours even better than Abby's?

intimacy and relationships are consistently deepening, where everything is improving. Women tend to feel that it's reasonable to expect more love and joy *this* year than they observed in the house *last* year. Women want more fulfilling married love *this* quarter than *last* quarter.

Likewise, what your wife probably wants most for you at work is not growth, but stability. If you worry about job security, she knows, you'll have a difficult time cultivating growth at home. Even if she works forty hours in the field or the office, too, a wife and mother still tends to be more concerned about growth in the home corporation.

In short, *you* thought you left work to come home, relax, regroup. *She* thinks you left work to come home to go to work—as a father and husband. Is it any wonder conflicts often arise?

Yet there is common ground. Acting intentionally starts by accepting a role of leadership in your home and family. Evaluate your home life as though you had just been made the company's new president. Assess the organization's mission statement. What goals will lead your family toward the fulfillment of that mission?

When you realize your significance at home and begin to act intentionally there, your stability won't be diminished—it will actually grow. For at home as well as in your corporation, people are your most important asset. When both employees and management are excited about what's happening—when production is up and everyone feels ownership in the process, the result is both growth *and* stability.

But consider this. If you ran your business affairs with the same amount of forethought and planning that you give to running your family, would you go out of business within six months? Too many of us play just defense in our families for years, simply expecting that things will work out fine at home without any particular plan in mind. Is it any wonder that marriages and families are either falling apart or are mediocre at best?

Simply put, your success as a father depends on your intentional actions.

The Five Lug Nuts

Each of these five lug nuts represents an aspect of acting intentionally. If one lug nut is loose or missing, you probably won't notice. The others carry the stress. Even if two are loose, you are still probably safe. But if three or more lug nuts are loose or missing,

Five Key Habits of Smart Dads
FATHERING PARADIGM

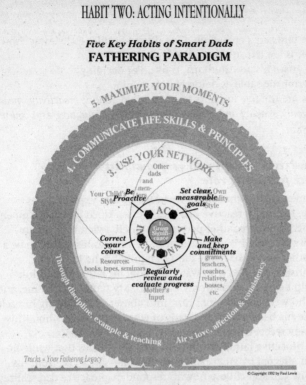

Tracks = Your Fathering Legacy

© Copyright 1992 by Paul Lewis

you are in grave danger. Sooner or later—and no telling when—one of those stressed studs will snap and you lose a wheel. By the same token, you don't have to immediately master all five aspects of acting intentionally as a father. If you tighten down just *some* of these lug nuts, you can proceed with confidence.

It's as easy to check your lifestyle for whether you're practicing intentional actions as it is to pop the hubcaps off your car and check the lug nuts. As a rim would eventually rattle off the axle with loose lug nuts, so the best of fathering practices fall apart without intentional actions. Without intentional actions, sound principles of fathering are about as useful as an unmounted wheel. When you act intentionally, however, the rest of your fathering habits take off and you reach your destination.

Concluding the discussion below of each lug nut is a way to immediately start tightening down the lug nut. These aren't mere postscripts, but vital steps toward changing as a father. In his video *Hooked on Life*, Stephen Arterburn offers this rid-

Smart Thought:
I can't do anything about my ancestors, but I can do a lot about my descendants.

dle: Five birds are perched on a log. If one decides to fly away, how many birds are left sitting on the log?

The answer, says Arterburn, is five. For deciding to do something is not the same as doing it.

Here are the five lug nuts of intentional action: *proactivity, measurable goals, making and keeping commitments, evaluation,* and *course correction.*

Lug Nut 1
Be proactive—accept full responsibility for your fathering role.

Let me explain what *proactive* means by first explaining its opposite, *reactive.* A reactive dad sees himself ruled by what happens in his life. A reactive father perceives himself a victim of circumstance. By blaming his circumstances, he excuses his failure to be a better father and to have the kind of family life he idealizes.

For instance, a dad who was abused by *his* father may think, I can't help being rough with my children. My father abused me, and those who were abused often turn into abusers. By allowing himself to excuse his behavior on the basis of what happened to him, this dad merely reacts without exercising his power of choice.

The proactive father, on the other hand, realizes that while he has been affected by what happened to him—say, abuse from his father—he can still choose how to respond. A proactive dad realizes that some men, abused by their fathers, in turn abuse their own children. But a proactive dad chooses to respond differently. Even if he was abused himself as a child, he can begin therapy to heal the effects of the abuse. He can take parenting classes.

The proactive father refuses to let what happens (or happened) to him rule his life. He does not let either the present or the past dictate the future.

When you are a proactive father, you choose your response to problems so that you can fulfill your fathering responsibilities. You control your life for your purposes. Although you cannot control what comes your way in life, you can control how you let it affect you.

Suppose you accept full responsibility for being a good father. You also know how important it is to spend time with your children. Although you don't set your work schedule, because you are proactive, you use your creativity and power of choice to devise ways to spend time with your children.

This could mean, of course, not taking up golf until the last child leaves for college. But you accept this as a reasonable tradeoff. The proactive dad does not beg off with the excuse, "You know I'd *like* to spend time with my children, but with my schedule I just can't." Instead, you'll focus on the minutes you do have and make the most of them.

Proactive fathers speak a different language than reactive fathers. The reactive father's vocabulary is replete with "I can't . . . I have to . . . I can't help it . . . I must . . ." The proactive father, on the other hand, uses phrases like "I can . . . I want to . . . I will . . . I choose to . . . I am not doomed to repeat the past . . . No one can take away my power to choose my response . . . When opportunity doesn't knock, I will build a door . . . I may not be able to control what happens, but I can control how I manage around what happens."

It can seem easier to be reactive. You will always find someone to blame for your failures and frustrations. And being proactive— accepting full responsibility for your life—means you have to seriously ponder the effects your decisions have on others.

A proactive father shelves all the excuses, instead confronting challenges head on. He believes his true priorities will determine the course of his life, because he is tenaciously deciding to keep those priorities in line.

Granted, accepting full responsibility for your fathering can be intimidating—but it can free you, too. All the time I hear fathers say they feel trapped. "I want to be a good father," they complain, "but I just don't know what it takes. I wish I had more time [money, energy, whatever], but the pressures of daily life keep me from being the kind of dad my kids need."

He may be genuinely trapped in a despicable job at the moment, or engulfed in debt and unable to spend the time or money his children need. But he is a free man when he can say, "I may not have much money, education, or free time—but whatever I have, I will manage so that my kids are taken care of." Risking failure, he still tries, he still accepts the challenge of managing his own life and resources in a way that displays his love for his wife and children. This determination gives him power the reactive man will never have.

Now tighten down the lug nut of proactivity: Practice five-minute fathering.

You don't need large chunks of time. Lots of things can be done in just five minutes. In just five minutes, you can—

- **Have a wonderful discussion about your child's best and worst moments at school today.**

Smart Idea:
A big cardboard appliance box can be the most entertaining toy you've brought home in a long time. Drop by an appliance store on your way home and ask for one.

- Hug your child (hang on for a whole minute) and tell her how important she is to your family.
- Write a letter of appreciation to his teacher for taking special care with him in the classroom.
- Share a dish of ice cream.
- Wrestle.
- Have an impromptu pillow fight.
- Give your child a sincere compliment.
- Play freeze tag.
- Write and give your child a little note.
- Leave for work five minutes later and spend that time with your children.
- Dissect the values in a TV program or news report you've watched together.
- Read a picture book.
- Say a prayer for your child.
- Stop somewhere on your way home from work long enough
to shift gears mentally and emotionally from
work to your family.

You get the idea. Make a list on a three-by-five card of five-minute activities that appeal most to you. Carry the card with you, and during spare moments do one of them. If you make this a habit, over the course of a lifetime you will have created countless memories of a father's love.

Lug Nut 2
Set clear, measurable goals for fathering.

A proactive father naturally sets goals, because goals are the way he accomplishes anything he wants in life, whether in fathering, business, sports, finances, or whatever. When you realize you are responsible for what happens, you tend to make sure the *right things* happen. This is where measurable goals come in. You measure what is, measure what you want, and then take action to shorten the distance between the two.

In our survey of fathers, we asked what advice they would give a new father. A majority recommended goal setting, with responses like these:

- Set and achieve family goals.
- Be goal-directed and help kids set goals.
- Set goals, establish a plan, check your progress.

- **Set proper goals and work as though all things depended on those goals.**
- **Be goal oriented.**[1]

It's good advice. Clear and measurable goals enable you to better use what time you do have with your children. With clearly defined goals, you will seize opportunities you might otherwise miss. Just the act of setting goals can spur your creativity toward reaching them.

For example:

You want to set clear, measurable goals about conveying your family's values to your children. You give the subject some thought, then write down the values you want to communicate—hard work, honesty, education. Now you keep your eyes open for natural opportunities to highlight these values to your children. Daniel is working hard at his homework, you notice, so you praise him not only for his effort, but for his wisdom in recognizing the value of hard work. When you catch Kristi in a fib, instead of getting angry you take the opportunity to stress the importance of honesty in building trust in relationships. Sara is impressed with a newscast about the space shuttle, and you see your chance to explain that the astronauts' education has paved their career path for them into space.

Without clear goals for conveying particular values to your children, one easily overlooks such teachable moments.

But relationships don't lend themselves to goal setting, some fathers tell me—at least like more concrete and practical matters do, such as raising sales figures or saving money for a boat. So I have listed below some of the fathering goals our survey turned up. We asked dads, "What are the three most important goals you have for your relationship with your children?"

Interaction Goals

- **That they know I love them.**
- **That we can talk about everything.**
- **That we trust each other.**

Personal Goals as a Father

- **To always be there when they need me.**

Smart Idea:

On your next business trip, if you can't take one of the kids with you, tape record yourself reading a few bedtime stories for your children to listen to while you're gone. Leave the books with them, so they can follow along as they listen to your tape. Spice up your recorded readings by making a funny or unusual noise when it's time to turn the page.

- To be a good listener.
- To be a positive role model.
- To be a good father.

Personal Goals for my Children

- That they have good self-esteem.
- That they contribute significantly to society.
- That they become good citizens.
- That they be hard workers.

Spiritual Goals

- To help them make spiritual commitments.
- To help them understand and achieve God's will for their lives.
- To be a good spiritual leader in my home.
- To train my children for spiritual leadership.

Experiential Goals

- To have time to play what they want to play.
- To be able to share activities with them.
- To learn to play together and enjoy each others' interests.
- To enjoy doing things together.
- To share an interest in some fun activity.[2]

If you want your goals to be useful, make sure they are measurable. Actually, some of the above goals are wishes, not goals. (How will a dad know when he and his child "trust each other"?) If you must, go ahead and *start* with wishes—just make sure that you define them clearly in measurable terms. Then take that measurable goal and fit it into a time frame—a thirteen-week quarter or a year—so that you can anticipate what progress you will have made ninety days from now, or a year from now.

For example, take the goal "that we trust each other." You can clarify it and make it measurable by breaking it down this way:

- List each promise you have already made your child; then, setting calendar deadlines for each one, do your best to fulfill your promises.
- Commend your child whenever she keeps her word. Discipline her whenever she acts in an untrustworthy fashion. If you keep notes about these incidents over a quarter, you can look back and evaluate her progress.
- Make only those commitments you can realistically keep.

By clarifying your desires and making them measurable, you create fathering goals you can later evaluate.

This process works only if you write your goals on your regular to-do list and tie it to your schedule and calendar like your business goals. Set your measurable goals in a limited time frame: I suggest setting fathering goals for ninety days at a time. Ninety days, a quarter, thirteen weeks, the length of a season—I believe this is the ideal planning time for seeing results. A quarter is long enough to get an overview (a monthly view is usually too short to observe the rhythmic fluctuations of life), but short enough for you to identify specific actions and assign them to particular days and weekends during which you will act on them.

Now tighten down the lug nut of measurable goals: Write some. Now.

Start by writing your desires for fathering—then turn those desires into measurable goals. Think in terms of personal goals, goals about what you want to teach your children, family vacations you want to take before they leave home, and so on.

Pull your family in on your dreaming, too. Set aside an evening or a long dinner out in a relatively quiet corner booth at your favorite pizza place. Ask family members, one at a time, to list what they want to accomplish in the next twelve months. Dream together. Write down each of their goals, and discuss how the whole family can help each person reach his or her goals.

(Part of the rationale behind this pizza night is that sharing goals and dreams always brings a family closer together. It's no wonder that such commitment to one another, along with time spent together, are two of the most common characteristics researchers have consistently noted in strong families.)

Smart Idea:
Whatever your children's ages, they always enjoy back rubs and foot rubs— plus they create an excellent climate for honest communication (especially foot rubs, which allow eye contact during dialogue).

Now organize your goals by the calendar. Big goals may take one, five, or ten years to accomplish. Others can be reached within a week or two. In any case, the secret is to break down a goal into practical, manageable steps. Then write those onto your calendar, because only what's written on your calendar or to-do lists will you most likely accomplish. What is not written down tends to float and will never be accomplished.

Consider using ninety days—the length of a season—as your planning window. To get specific, ask yourself questions like this:

1. In what way do I want my relationship with my wife and each of my children to be different or better in ninety days from what it is today?

2. In what way do I want my fathering practices to change?

3. What are direct action steps I could take that would lead me toward these desires? On what actual calendar week and/or day will I take each of these steps?

Few things will sharpen your focus as a father more than writing down such answers on paper and then acting on your plan. On page 92 is a blank 90-Days Family Goals Sheet. A filled-in sample is also provided on page 93.

Now translate your ninety-day plan into weekly and daily activity calendars and to-do lists. On page 94 is a Weekly Plan Sheet that integrates family plans with your business and other time commitments.

As you lay out a week, first trace down the vertical shaded column for that week on your 90-Day Family Plan Sheet. Under the "Marriage/Family" heading in the lower left corner of the Weekly Plan Sheet, list the items you planned to include in that particular week.

Block out time for each activity in that week's plan so that other urgencies don't crowd out your family and fathering priorities. You've allotted the time, so now guard it as you do any other appointment.

When you have sketched out where your family fits in the week's plans, do one more thing: Take your appointment book to the dinner table tonight. Show each member of your family the unassigned times in your schedule over the next week or two, then write in their names at times you all agree upon. (Remember—it is not enough to make the commitment. It only counts if you keep the commitments you make.)

Smart Tip:
Read your high schooler's textbooks. You'll never be at a loss for a good conversation topic.

As you plan your day each morning or the evening before, again bring from your Weekly Plan Sheet the fathering and family activities that are scheduled for that day and slot them into the day as precisely as possible. The principle that daily moves the business world also works to your advantage in your family: only what you write on your calendar or "to do" lists will you consistently achieve.

Lug Nut 3
Make and keep commitments that help you fulfill fathering goals.

Commitments about your time, for example. The good Lord gives everyone on the planet 24 hours a day, 168 hours in the week. You are responsible for how you use your time. If you do not consciously choose how to spend your time, others will make the choices for you. One way or another, a choice is always made; because unless you die within the next 24 hours, you will use up the time allotted to you this day.

We commit time to work, to rest, to eating and sleeping, grooming and recreation—the essentials. Then there's discretionary time—and our use of it reflects our priorities and values. (The same holds true for discretionary money, energy, talents, patience, and so on.)

Without an intelligent plan for time management—and your *commitment* to it—you are merely drifting with the wind instead of steering yourself where you want to be as a father. And to drift in your fathering is to eventually face the consequences of not committing to a deliberate plan.

But I have no control over my schedule, protests the reactive man. Yet the proactive man sets goals and priorities, choosing to commit his time and resources toward achieving them. He may not reach half of them, but he will reach *some*—and steady though slight progress inevitably leads to the goal.

Here's one way to make clear fathering commitments: Set aside a regular time for previewing days and weeks. Plan your fathering week on Friday or Saturday or Sunday—whichever day is the eve of your "week." Similarly, plan each day that morning or—better yet—the evening before. You'll find that you control your time better by consistently giving it to those events that matter most to you. "To fail to plan is to plan to fail," goes the maxim—and it is as absolutely true in fathering as in most other arenas of life. You must direct your resources in advance to where you want them to go.

However simple the event you schedule with your children, put it on the calendar and guard it as you do other important dates. Don't trust to chance for communicating your love and support on a regular basis to your kids. *Schedule* opportunities to say or demonstrate your love for them. It's not as important what you do together as long as you commit the time, then guard it and spend it as you planned. "I wish earlier I would have learned to schedule time with

90-Day Family Goals

Goal	Steps to Fulfillment	Week of:
My fathering practices		
Relationship with (wifes name)		
Relationship with (child's name)		
Relationship with (child's name)		
Relationship with (child's name)		
Relationship with (child's name)		
Relationship with (child's name)		

90-Day Family Goals

Goal	Steps to Fulfillment	Week of: JAN 3 / 10 / 17 / 24 — FEB 2 / 9 / 16 / 23 — MAR 2 / 9 / 16 / 23 / 30
My fathering practices		
CONSISTENT PLANNING	Weekly 15 min review	～～～～
JOURNALING	Write down experiences	X X X X X X
TIME/CONTACT W/ DAD	Weekly phone + 2 visits	～X～～X～→
Relationship with (wife's name) KAREN		
Read 1 Book together	"Marriage passages"	～～
Sharpen tennis game	Clinic @ Community Center	X
Plan anniversary getaway	Book hotel, arr. babysit	X ⊗
Relationship with (child's name) MEGAN		
TIGHTEN COMMUNICATION	Breakfast Tuesdays	～
FOCUS ON LIFE GOALS	Start notebook – 3 topics	X (#1) (#2) (#3)
Relationship with (child's name) RICHARD		
SCOUTING TOGETHER	Select troop & enroll	～→ X
BUILD HOMEWORK SKILLS	Set-up place / tools	X ～～～
Relationship with (child's name) PETER		
READ FANTASY BOOKS	C.S. Lewis – 3x week	～～～～
INVOLVE IN CHORES	Help w/ fence repair / paint	X →
Relationship with (child's name) JANET		
ENCOURAGE!	1 note / letter / card a week	～～～
PLAN SUMMER TRIP	Clear calendars, get info	X → X
Relationship with (child's name) JON		
EST. FINANCIAL ORG.	Launch checking act.	X ～→ Review
DISCIPLE DISCUSS.	Bi-weekly breakfast.	X X X X X X X

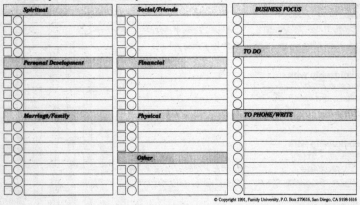

© Copyright 1991, Family University, P.O. Box 279616, San Diego, CA 9198-1616

my children," admits Josh McDowell in the video *Famous Fathers*. "If I don't schedule the time, I don't get it."

Without this lug nut firmly tightened down, you may not leave the imprint you want on your children's lives. When you learn the habit of making and keeping commitments to your children, you build in them a trust that will give them inner security throughout life.

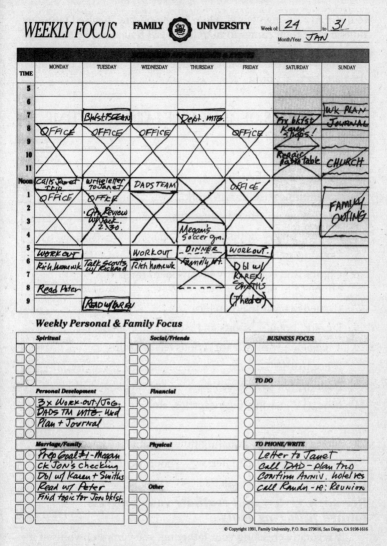

WEEKLY FOCUS   FAMILY 🎓 UNIVERSITY   Week of: 24 to 31

Month/Year JAN

TIME	MONDAY	TUESDAY	WEDNESDAY	THURSDAY	FRIDAY	SATURDAY	SUNDAY
5							
6							
7		Bkfst Steen		Dept. mtg.		Fix bkfst	WK PLAN / JOURNAL
8	OFFICE	OFFICE	OFFICE		OFFICE	Karen Shops!	
9							
10						Repair patio table	CHURCH
11							
Noon	Calls Janet Trip	write letter To Janet	DADS TEAM		OFFICE		
1	OFFICE	OFFICE					FAMILY OUTING
2		Qtr Review w/Jack 2:30					
3							
4				Megan's Soccer gym.			
5	WORKOUT		WORKOUT	DINNER	WORKOUT		
6	Rich homewk	Talk Scouts w/ Richard	Rich homewk	family nt.	Dbl w/ KAREN, SMITHS		
7							
8	Read Peter				(Theater)		
9		READ w/ KAREN					

Weekly Personal & Family Focus

Spiritual
- ☐ ○
- ☐ ○
- ☐ ○
- ☐ ○

Personal Development
- ☐ ○ 3x WORK-out/Jog.
- ☐ ○ DADS TM mtg. Wed
- ☐ ○ Plan + Journal

Marriage/Family
- ☐ ○ Prep Goal #1 - Megan
- ☐ ○ Ck Jon's checking
- ☐ ○ Dbl w/ Karen + Smiths
- ☐ ○ Read w/ Peter
- ☐ ○ Find topic for Jon bkfst.

Social/Friends
- ☐ ○
- ☐ ○
- ☐ ○
- ☐ ○

Financial
- ☐ ○
- ☐ ○
- ☐ ○
- ☐ ○

Physical
- ☐ ○

Other
- ☐ ○
- ☐ ○
- ☐ ○

BUSINESS FOCUS
- ○
- ○
- ○

TO DO
- ○
- ○
- ○
- ○
- ○

TO PHONE/WRITE
- ○ Letter to Janet
- ○ Call DAD - plan trip
- ○ Confirm Anniv. hotel res
- ○ Call Randy - re: Reunion

© Copyright 1991, Family University, P.O. Box 279616, San Diego, CA 91981616

Now tighten down the lug nut of making and keeping commitments: Make some—now—and determine to keep them.

On the form on page 96 take five minutes to inventory your time spent. Add up your total, subtract it from 168 hours—the amount available to every one of us every week—and see what's left to distribute among your children in one-on-one, focused fathering time. If your total comes to more than 168 hours (as I've seen happen), you now know why you've been feeling so pinched for time. Look for where you want to cut your commitments, and then do the hard part: Act on it.

168 HOURS OF AVAILABLE FATHERING TIME

Estimated Hours Per Week

1. On the job, at the office, etc. ...._____

2. Commuting to and from work..._____

3. Drive times to other destinations......................................._____

4. Sleeping (avg. 7 hours per day) ...._____

5. Dressing, personal hygiene..._____

6. Church and community involvement (meetings, phone calls, practice, games, etc.)...................................._____

7. Home/lawn/car maintenance..._____

8. Errands, hobbies, sports and recreation, exercise, etc........_____

9. Time alone with wife (or serious relationships, if not married).._____

10. Reading, bill paying, etc. ...._____

11. Misc. (TV viewing, business trips, etc.) ...._____

    Subtotal   _____

12. Maximum family/fathering time available per week........._____

    Divided by ____ children = ____hours per child per week

Lug Nut 4
Regularly review and evaluate your progress toward fathering goals.

By regularly checking your fathering, you can catch yourself if you get headed in a wrong direction. Even if you're being diligent, your approach may be off base. With the feedback you receive from evaluating your progress, you can correct your course.

If you regularly come up short on your objectives, something's wrong. Let these repeated failures prompt an investigation of *why* you are failing. Maybe you lack a particular fathering skill. Maybe you're overcommitted and should eliminate or rearrange elements in your schedule to make your objectives realistic. Maybe you're good at setting clear plans and objectives for your family, but your behavior doesn't follow your professed priorities.

Denial is the plague of honest evaluation. Be willing to admit that, in reality, your supposedly critical objectives may not actually be so critical to you. When you admit this, you can actually begin changing and doing what *is* critical to you. Make change a one-step-at-at-time process. Efforts at wholesale change usually fail.

As well as plan the next day and week ahead of time, I try to *review* my fathering goals week by week, too. What worked? What didn't work? Furthermore, I *revise* my fathering goals quarterly. (Again, a quarterly review gives me enough time to detect trends, but not so much lag time that attempts at course correction are too late.) Try planning your quarterly fathering reviews to coincide with the change of the seasons—if not according to the exact solstices and equinoxes, then maybe these more natural seasonal markers instead: the first day of your kids' school year; Thanksgiving; Easter or your kids' spring break; and the beginning of their summer vacation. Or follow your company's quarterly review schedule.

Visionary men especially need to evaluate their fathering, because although they're great goal setters, they're lousy at recognizing what it takes to reach those goals. I know—I'm one of them. If you're like me, you have to be particularly careful to set *realistic* goals. And you have to be equally careful and realistic in your self-evaluation.

Suppose you want to spend more time in meaningful conversation with each of your children. To make this a goal, you start by realistically measuring the time you now spend talking with them. I suggest getting an *objective* measure of the status quo—like noting each evening how much conversation you had that day. Then, with a realistic assessment in hand, you know what you're measuring against and if you're improving.

This is no throw-away issue. A Gallup survey conducted for the National Center for Fathering asked fathers, mothers, and their adult children how much time the fathers spent talking with their children each day. The fathers estimated 2.3 hours per day; mothers, 2.0 hours; and the adult children, 1.5 hours.[3] Other research suggests that most fathers spend far less time even than this in

> **Smart Idea:**
> Make a habit of taking your child to breakfast once a month. That adds up to 144 conversations over twelve years.

meaningful conversation with their children. The average father has 2.7 encounters with his six-year-old and younger children per day, each encounter lasting an average of fifteen seconds. That's an average of only forty seconds per child per day of meaningful conversation. As his kids grow up, another study suggests, fathers get better at talking with them—but not much better. From a statistically valid and anonymous survey of more than a thousand teenagers during the summer of 1987, it was found that the average teenager during a typical week spends less than *fifteen minutes* in meaningful conversation with his or her father.[4]

So start your evaluation process by objectively measuring if it's fifteen minutes a *day* or a *week* you're currently spending with your child. The revelation may alarm you, but only then can you set a realistic goal—and later celebrate your actual, instead of imagined, progress.

Now tighten down the lug nut of evaluation: Plan to review and evaluate your progress.

Examine your calendar. Identify four hours or so sometime about ninety days from today. Schedule a time and place where you can review and evaluate your progress without interruption. Guard this time as zealously as you would a corporate planning retreat. Although it is easy to get started with enthusiasm, you need a firm date and place reserved so that you will carry on as intended three months from now.

Lug Nut 5
Correct your course as necessary to reach fathering goals.

There are no perfect fathers, which is to say that even the best fathers constantly correct their courses along the way. Whether you're setting too many goals or unrealistic goals, course correction lets you compensate for this.

Smart Idea: Get some sleep even when a teenager is out late. Set your alarm for the curfew hour. If they get home before the deadline they can shut it off—and wake you, if you want. Otherwise the alarm will alert you to a missed curfew.

Several years ago I heard a successful, busy surgeon explain a routine that kept his marriage happy. He habitually spent the first twenty minutes at home each day in his rocking chair off the kitchen. When he was in that chair, he intentionally gave his wife his full attention while they discussed the personal and family issues on their minds that day.

When I heard that, I thought it was a smart idea. So I made it a goal of mine, too. The trouble was, I had younger children with their own ideas of what my agenda should be when I walked in the door at night—and it didn't include leaving Daddy alone for twenty minutes so he could sit in a chair and talk with their mom. It may have been a great plan for the doc, but despite repeated efforts, it soon became clear that it wouldn't work for me. I had to correct my course and move to a pattern of bedtime or early-morning chats with Leslie when the children were asleep. Someday I'd like to try the twenty-minute chats when I return home. The idea still appeals to me.

When I sail—which I love to do—I can point a sailboat directly where I want to go. But because I cannot control the wind, rarely do I get to sail a beeline to my destination. Instead, I have to tack, zigzag fashion, to reach my mark.

Fathering is the same. Circumstances interfere with my perfect plans, making a straight course impossible to travel.

When you find yourself off course, says motivational speaker Zig Ziglar, "you don't change your decision to go. You change your direction to get there."

That's good fathering advice. When circumstances blow you off course, reaffirm your commitment to your children, refocus on your goals, and figure out how to get back on course.

Now tighten down the lug nut of course correction: Do it regularly and often.

Throughout each day, whenever you preview and review your week—and especially when you review your progress after ninety days—correct your course as necessary.

Holding It All Together

Acting intentionally empowers you to be the best dad you can be regardless of your current limitations. Acting intentionally allows you to dream of your fathering ideals and yet be realistic enough to consistently take small, simple, and steady steps toward your dreams.

A set of lug nuts doesn't make a wheel, and acting intentionally is only one of the five key habits of a smart dad. But the lug nuts of intentional action hold it all together.

Now let's look at the rim, and we'll identify more resources for making you a great father.

7

Habit Three: Using Your Network
The Rim

In a Calvin and Hobbes cartoon, the diminutive imp hands his father a document. "Here, Dad," he says. "I'd like you to sign this form and have it notarized."

His dad reads the paper: "I, the undersigned dad, attest that I have never parented before, and insofar as I have no experience in the job, I am liable for my mistakes and I agree to pay for any counseling, in perpetuity, Calvin may require as a result of my parental ineptitude."

In the final frame, a disgruntled Calvin sits on his bed, muttering, "I don't see how you're allowed to have a kid without signing one of those."

Whether or not Calvin's dad is as inept as his little gargoyle of a son thinks he is, fathers nevertheless worry about it. They have few reality checks against which to compare their fathering decisions or style. They generally work out their fathering issues, like most issues, in isolation—without good models, without strategies, without support. Until recently, it seems, men did not converse openly about how to be a good father. Most simply tried to do their best, without help from outside themselves. Though sometimes I lament (with tongue in cheek) that fathering couldn't be more like football—with special teams and players to cover every situation—good fathering actually does resemble football in this detail: fathering was meant to be a team effort, not an isolated struggle.

Why a Network?

If it is true that no man is an island, then it follows that no man should behave as an island if he wants to be a strong father. Island living is a sign of strength, some men believe. Yet it doesn't take too many years of fathering to realize that the job really wasn't designed to be done alone.

Consider how the creator designed human reproduction—it requires both a man and a woman, together, to create a child. This is at least an indication that raising children is a team effort from the get-go. Finding and using a support network for fathering will be easier for you, of course, if your job or pastime requires teamwork. If you work alone, on the other hand, it will take more getting used to.

In any case, a network is as necessary to your fathering as a strong rim is to your tire's performance.

Rugged individualism is a hallmark of American history and folklore. Although most men probably understand that they can benefit from a network, far too many cultural messages have sent us packing in the opposite direction. In *The Seven Habits of Highly Effective People*, Stephen Covey notes that the current social paradigm enthrones independence. It is the avowed goal of many individuals and social movements. Most of the self-improvement material puts independence on a pedestal, as though communication, teamwork, and cooperation were lesser values.

But much of our current emphasis on independence is a reaction to dependence—to having others control us, define us, use us, and manipulate us. The little-understood concept of interdependence appears to many to smack of dependence, and therefore, we find people, often for selfish reasons, leaving their marriages, abandoning their children, and forsaking all kinds of social responsibility—all in the name of independence.[1]

Smart Idea:

Next month cash your paycheck in one-dollar bills. When you get home, pile them on the table along with the month's bills to be paid. Ask each child to count out the mortgage payment, car payment, utility and phone bills, and amounts for food, gas, and clothes— just to graphically illustrate for your children that the family operates on finite funds.

HABIT THREE: USING YOUR NETWORK

Although cultural messages still applaud independence, it is nevertheless becoming more acceptable for men to reach out and ask for fathering advice—perhaps because a record proportion of this decade's fathers were raised at least part of their lives without live-in fathers. Common sense alone dictates that if a boy doesn't have a role model, he needs to find some as a man.

Five Key Habits of Smart Dads
FATHERING PARADIGM

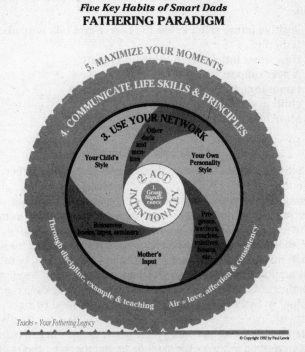

Tracks = Your Fathering Legacy

© Copyright 1992 by Paul Lewis

Most dads in Dads University seminars already generally recognize their need for a network. After all, they *did* sign up to attend a fathering course. So when they are asked, "What would help you to be a better father?" their answers echo a need for network—either a primary network (the father, his child, and his wife or the child's mother) or a secondary network (other fathers, other significant adults, and inanimate resources).

"What would help you to be a better father?"

- **Knowing my children**
- **More time together with family**
- **More quality time together**
- **Being more direct in communicating with my teens**

- Developing a conflict-free marriage
- Being more considerate of others in my family
- Improving my relationship with others
- More help from my wife
- More time with my wife

"What help from resources outside your immediate family would you like?"

- Positive father role models to observe and talk with about fathering
- How other fathers have solved problems
- A peer support group of fathers
- Counseling with someone who has studied child psychology
- More information and input on fatherhood[2]

Using Your Network

Cultivate a network of support relationships for your fathering—one or two, four or five friends with whom you can exchange fathering discoveries and frustrations and questions, and from whom you can ask for advice when you need it—especially from a man who is a little ahead of you on the fathering road. Talking about adolescence with someone who has already fathered his way through his child's adolescence, for instance, can give you both moral support and insight into that season of parenting. Reading the findings of one who has studied discipline, sibling rivalry, or parenting styles can give you the knowledge you need to make wise decisions.

Start building your network with a simple phone call to a friend, or a conversation in the locker room or around the water cooler. "Jim, one thing I admire about you is the common sense you seem to apply to your family life—you know, just what you do as a dad. I'm not sure about some of the calls I've made in my family. Would you be interested in getting together from time to time to talk openly about scaling the walls I come up against trying to be a good dad? I know *I'd* sure benefit from that kind of interaction. Maybe Bill would be interested in joining in, too."

Set a time and place to meet, and start with the idea that you'll get together at least three times in the first five or six weeks for continuity and true support to take place in the relationships.

You can function at one of three levels, writes Stephen Covey in *The Seven Habits of Highly Effective People*—in dependence, independence, or interdependence. And he makes a strong case for interdependency:

> Dependent people need others to get what they want. Independent people can get what they want through their own efforts. Interdependent people combine their own efforts with the efforts of others to achieve their greatest success.[3]

When I function as an interdependent person, man, and father, I look for and regularly gain the opportunity to tap the vast experience, wisdom, and potential that is resident in the fathering pilgrimage of other men. I am less afraid and more motivated to reveal my inner self to other men—and, in return, be rewarded by deeper levels of friendship. A network allows me to create synergy with others for greater success as a father than I could achieve acting independently.

Your Primary Network

Three relationships intersect to form your primary fathering network, similar to the dominant spokes in a high-performance wheel rim:

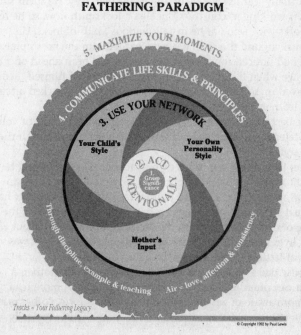

Five Key Habits of Smart Dads
FATHERING PARADIGM

5. MAXIMIZE YOUR MOMENTS

4. COMMUNICATE LIFE SKILLS & PRINCIPLES

3. USE YOUR NETWORK

Your Child's Style

Your Own Personality Style

2. ACT INTENTIONALLY

1. Grasp Significance

Mother's Input

Through discipline, example & teaching

Air = love, affection & consistency

Tracks = Your Fathering Legacy

© Copyright 1992 by Paul Lewis

onality, style, and talents
's personality, style, talents, and development
mother's input and support

tions of these personalities prompt various respons- some of his children's traits, a father must realize, simply don't mesh with his. This apparent conflict doesn't mean that one personality is better than the other. The smart dad simply notes the differences, then finds ways to accommodate them—while still affirming the person his child was created to be.

Of my five children, Jon is least like me. He cares little about convention and what people think of him. As a youngster he never wanted me to show him how to do anything. Jon was always confident he could figure it out for himself. My fantasies of Norman Rockwell moments with him never came to pass. Jon didn't want to be taught woodworking. Before I could finish my little lecture about the safe use of the rotary sander, he'd grab it or else he'd walk away saying, "Okay, okay, I got it!" The difference between our personalities caused many tense moments over the years.

Yet I eventually learned to appreciate Jon's learning style, and he eventually learned woodworking in his own way. He spent some summers working in construction. He's a locksmith now, so he regularly works with wood as he installs various kinds of locks. His woodwork around the shop has even earned him the boss's praise.

If I had noticed sooner that Jon always had been ahead of others his age when it came to taking responsibility for himself, I could have saved myself a lot of frustration. I should have backed off and let Jon learn as he learns best.

The best parenting strategy is a difficult one: take note of your child's talents and adapt your training methods to mesh with the child's style.

After Jon moved out to his own apartment, I asked him if he wanted to meet for breakfast once a week to talk. Now over pancakes or oatmeal, our love and mutual respect for one another has deepened more as adult friends than as father and son. With the passing of only a couple years, our freedom to comment about each other's lives and to swap advice has changed completely. It was a matter of letting Jon be Jon.

A wise dad also listens to the input of the child's mother. A woman can often read a child's emotional condition more readily, or be more aware of what is typical behavior—if for no other reason than spending more time with her child than a father typically does. Leslie has abundant intuition when it comes to our children. She naturally has a different perspective of her children than I do—a maternal view that is an asset to me when I listen to her insight.

This primary network is dynamic; that is, it exists in motion, not at rest. At the office, on the other hand, relationships and boundaries and interactions tend to be more static. You typically have a designated work space, clear job expectations, and well-worn paths of communication with those above and below you in corporate hierarchy.

At home, however, boundaries tend to be fuzzy. Yet men tend to continue operating at home the way they did at the office, especially if they do not know themselves well. Such fathers run over other family members without respecting their differences. They don't recognize their blind spots.

Only when you respect your child and the mother as much as yourself can you take what each personality brings to your domestic mix, and from it help shape a pattern of mutual support.

Your Personality, Style, and Talents

It is in their work that men tend to express their personality, style, and talents most intensely. Although fathering is primarily relational, most men see it, too, as a job. So when you consider how you handle most jobs, you can see how your personality carries over into your fathering style as well.

Some guys are hands-on managers, some like to delegate, some are naturally strong leaders, others are naturally strong background and support people. How you father will reveal your management style—and don't be surprised if your management style doesn't mesh with all of your children.

Suppose you're a take-charge leader with two kids, for instance—one is naturally docile, a follower. The other child is just like you, a born leader. As sure as your eyes are reading these words, your take-charge style will go head to head with whichever child inherited your personality. So you need to understand the styles of you and all your children; in this way you can manage and reduce conflicts. You will avoid approving the docile child simply because he does what you want without asking any questions, and you will find

Smart Idea:
Next holiday when the grandfolks visit, videotape an interview with them, during which each of them reminisces about their childhood experiences, their own parents, what their best and worst choices were, etc. The video will become an instant family heirloom.

ways to affirm your other child's grit while teaching him how to submit to authority.

"Fathering Confidence: Shaping Your Own Style" is the title of a Dads University half-day course, in which I teach a personal-assessment approach I call *historical intelligence*. It doesn't plot you on a preconceived axis or grid of personality types based on how you score compared to a set of standardized norms. It runs contrary to the feeling we've grown up with, that measurement and evaluation highlight only our mistakes—what we do wrong. With historical intelligence, we begin by assuming that everyone is born with a unique matrix of drives, gifts, and abilities. It is these we want to discover by evaluating the content of stories they select from a life of significant and satisfying achievements. Historical intelligence looks only to what we do well or right to form an assessment.

What Are Your Strengths?

Your natural abilities shine most at the times you've achieved the best in your life. Your interests and achievements tend to flow from your deepest natural ability, something you naturally focus on and do very well. These *inborn* talents and *natural* abilities differ from the skills you have *learned* and may, in fact, be very good at.

To assess your strengths using the historical-intelligence method, you analyze the content of your achievement stories—five to ten episodes and experiences in your life from childhood to the present that you remember fondly as your best and most satisfying moments. Even if the stories are different and disconnected, you will find that common threads run through them all. Dads University participants select and tell stories of past personal achievements. These stories we examine for the tell-tale signs of natural drives and abilities:

- **What are the central two or three dynamics that motivate a father most?**
- **What kind of stage (that is, circumstances) does this man prefer to play on?**
- **What kind of supporting cast does he prefer to have around him?**
- **What kind of applause does he enjoy most? Financial? Praise? Status?**
- **What pace does he tend to work at?**

Then we compare these findings (a father's natural abilities) to the requirements of fathering (the five key habits) and see exactly what he does naturally that is also smart fathering.

Just as you will probably be stressed out in a job that requires talents you *don't* have, yet has no use for qualities you possess in abundance—so fathering will be much easier if you know your personality, your style, and your natural abilities and subsequently play to your strengths. What you don't do well, you can fill in from your network (mother of child, other fathers, outside resources). You accentuate the positive and compensate for the negative. You play smarter, not harder.

When his twin daughters were old enough to eat solid food, Noel Paul Stookey (Paul of the folk-singing group Peter, Paul, and Mary) unsuccessfully tried to get the baby food from the jar and into the girls' mouths, which they clamped shut at the sight of a spoonful of Gerber's. Attached to one of the high-chair trays Paul noticed a rattle, wobbling on its suction-cup base. He pulled it off, stuck it on his forehead, and got the silly thing dancing wildly. Of course, his girls were so captivated by the gyrating rattle projecting out of their father's head (or so it seemed) that their mouths dropped open—which gave him time enough to spoon the meal into their mouths.

Stookey did no more than what you can do. He simply used his own personality style to accomplish his particular fathering challenges. And you can do it your way, with your style and your natural abilities.

Your Child's Personality, Style, Talents, and Development

As you make the most of your own natural style and abilities in leading your family, do the same for your children. Become a student of each of your children—really noticing what is unique to each one—so that you can make affirming comments every time your child does something well. This habit fosters healthy self-esteem in any child.

Plus you have to consider some other facets of your children.

Smart Idea:
After dinner one night this week, haul out the photo albums or video tapes and relive your best family vacation. Before you get too far into the vacation's photos or video, hold hands in a circle and —with eyes closed—try to storytell your way through each day in sequence.

• **Developmental stages.** Children grow through predictable stages of physical, mental, emotional, and moral development. If you know what stage a child is in, you won't inadvertently demand behavior of which the child is simply incapable. You don't ask a two-year-old to carry a forty-pound suitcase upstairs—which is akin to what we unfairly require sometimes in ways other than physical.

In children younger than two or so, for example, normal cognitive development has not progressed far enough to let them project *what might happen* to them—which is why, up to about this age, they are perfectly content to sleep in a pitch-dark room. As the brain develops, however, and the child grows into the next cognitive level, she begins to project *what might happen* to her in the dark. Almost overnight, it seems, she becomes afraid of the dark and begins squawking for a night light. Nor will it do any good to point out to her that just yesterday she was content sleeping in a dark room.

When you know your child's developmental stage, you can make better decisions about your child.

So open your calendar right now and schedule a forty-five minute visit to the library soon. Get your hands on some child-psychology books with developmental charts. Photocopy one or two you feel will be useful, and put them where you can refer to them every two or three months—or whenever a child does or says something that makes you wonder about just where he is developmentally.

• **Learning styles.** Like you, children also have individual learning styles. Some learn best by *hearing* information; others, by *seeing* it; still others, by getting their hands on it and working with it. Determine how your child prefers to learn—especially if she has a learning difficulty—for then you can present material in the manner she can best assimilate it.

My nine-year-old is strongly auditory. If you want David to do a list of chores, tell him—don't leave a note. He'll remember what you tell him, but he'll forget to check a list I've written out for him. In his schoolwork, reading a book is a less effective way of learning for David than listening to a teacher explain the same information—which is exactly the opposite of his sister's learning style.

When I cooperate with the different learning styles of my children, I get more results as a dad.[4]

The Child's Mother

Her role in your child's life is inestimable. You are wise to cooperate with her. Even if you and she do not live together, it is vital that you work together in the best interest of your child. If you *are* married to the child's mother, of course, this aspect of your network will be easier.

If you don't regularly do this, start now asking your child's mother for insight into your child's personality, style, and talents. Use questions such as, "What's the best way I can encourage Kim? At this time, what does she need most from me? Is there an immediate goal you are working on for which I can provide support? Can I help you by coming in from a different angle?"

Take it a step further: Ask her for her perspective of your own personality, style, and abilities as they relate to your fathering. Let her encourage and support you in your fathering. The feedback of someone who loves your child as much as you do is a resource you neglect only to your own detriment.

The Secondary Network

Your secondary network consists of other fathers, other players in your child's life, and outside resources that can be used to enhance your fathering.

Five Key Habits of Smart Dads
FATHERING PARADIGM

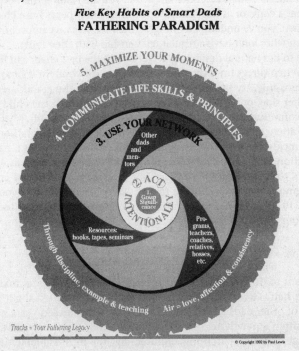

5. MAXIMIZE YOUR MOMENTS

4. COMMUNICATE LIFE SKILLS & PRINCIPLES

3. USE YOUR NETWORK

Other dads and mentors

2. ACT INTENTIONALLY

1. Grasp Significance

Resources: books, tapes, seminars

Programs, teachers, coaches, relatives, bosses, etc.

Through discipline, example & teaching

Air = love, affection & consistency

Tracks = Your Fathering Legacy

© Copyright 1992 by Paul Lewis

You need relationships with other fathers and mentors for your moral support, encouragement, and accountability. Mentors can also be a role model for *you*—something you may not have had as a child. Contact with other players in your child's life—teachers, coaches, club leaders—allows you to draw from their insight, knowledge, and awareness of your child as well as to monitor their influence on your child. Then there are resources outside your routine—material as well as people—than can fill in the fathering blanks.

A lot of divorced or separated fathers are in anguish when custody battles and unfriendly courts make contact with their children difficult or even impossible. There are no easy answers or solutions to this problem. The best advice I can give you is this:

• Call family-law attorneys, friends, psychologists—anyone you can think of for a referral to a fathers'-rights support group in your community. Discover whatever network they have of legal advice and resources.

• Let you child's mom know that, past history notwithstanding, you have no intention of giving up on having a good relationship with your child. As evidence, let her know that you are reading this book. Send her a copy, or at least photocopy for her a few pages from chapter five where you've underlined or highlighted the negative impact of children who don't have a regular relationship with their father. Appeal to her natural desire to give your child the best chance in life.

• When direct lines of communication with your child's mother are impossible, try tactfully staying in touch with the grandparents on either side, or with some other relative with which the child's mom communicates. Word of your love as a father can filter back.

• Patience is a crucial weapon. I've spoken with many fathers who quickly became discouraged and still remain angry. It's a natural reaction when you care so deeply and all the courts seem interested in is your child-support dollars. But time is on your side; if you will demonstrate your concern in any way you can, one day your child will begin thinking for himself or herself and will want to see you. Your dedication will be rewarded.

Other Fathers and Mentors

Want to double your fathering confidence and cut your anxieties in half? Get in the habit of meeting regularly with a small group of other dads to talk about fathering. For fourteen years now I've written a newsletter on fathering. I've read extensively about marriage, families, parenting, children. But the most valuable time

I've spent becoming a confident dad was in my weekly meetings with two other friends and fathers for an hour or two discussing our fathering skills and problems. At first we put a spin on our stories so we'd look good. But we quickly realized that omitting our ugly little details did no one any good. So to encourage each other to be honest, we agreed that any time one of us sensed the whole story wasn't being told, he had standing authorization to call the wife and get *her* version of the incident.

That took care of pretense.

We give each other freedom to ask hard questions of us—but that also help us become better fathers. In these discussions we've helped each other through daughters' boyfriends we didn't like, through children struggling to manage sexual values in school, media influences, poor attitudes, and problems about marital compatibility. We've watched each other's kids grow, and we've celebrated the victories along the way.

We don't meet as often now, but we still share a warmth and freedom on the phone or in person with each other that I don't easily have with other men. I wouldn't trade those hours for anything—sitting in a car, around a table in a mall restaurant, walking the trails at a nearby park. There's fathering power and safety in those relationships.

Every dad needs a group of men committed to his support. It creates a source of encouragement and feedback essential to maintaining the five key habits of smart dads.

Consider these ground rules for such a group:

• *Keep confidences.* What is said won't be repeated even to spouses, without explicit permission. Trust is impossible without confidentiality.

• *Don't gossip.* Be especially careful not to talk about group members in their absence.

• *Attend regularly.* How strictly you define "regular attendance" is up to your group. But keep in mind that casual attendance delays the development of the group and can frustrate more committed members. If you've asked for a commitment to a limited number of meetings—maybe six or eight—then regular attendance should be a reasonable expectation.

Smart Idea:
Collect in a folder, shoe box, or notebook all the quotes, clippings, anecdotes, and stories that best express your beliefs and favorite axioms. Label it "Ideas I Want My Kids to Remember," and organize the material as a going-away gift when they leave home.

• *Participate, but don't dominate.* Everyone has something to contribute, and no one has all the answers.

• *Accept disagreement.* Your purpose is not to see everything alike. You agree simply to disagree courteously.

Start your own fathering support group in two steps:

Step 1. Make a short list of dads with whom you enjoy talking—and who are committed to being good dads. Give each a call and, either on the phone or over lunch, explain what you're thinking about:

• You want to turn in a strong fathering performance, but you're not always sure what to do. As in other endeavors and business, you've found wisdom and strength in asking questions and getting wise counsel.

• You're looking for two or three or four fathers who would meet every week or two for ninety days to talk openly about fathering, family, and how to win the day-to-day fight to keep life in balance. You're looking for guys who could give and receive advice and hold each other accountable for carrying out plans the discussions might unfold.

• Ask for a commitment of six to eight weeks to see what value might unfold. Explain that you'll come prepared each time with a little agenda and some fathering information that can kick off a useful discussion. (Men are seldom motivated to carve out valuable time for a meeting with no agenda and no one in charge.)

Step 2. At your first get together, break the ice by asking each man to describe the differences between each of his children (their personality bents, interests, which parent they're most like, etc.). You go first, to demonstrate the detail and honesty you're expecting from each man.

Pass out photocopies of a short article about kids, families, or fathering you've found that raises good questions or offers advice. Read it together and talk about how it does or doesn't apply to each of your situations.

Assign simple homework for everybody based on conclusions you reached. Create a short list of topics you want to discuss next time. Review the ground rules for your group.

Once you're past a couple of meetings, close the group to new members so that you can build on the intimacy you've launched. You can invite others in when you restart the group or form a different group after a break from meeting.

A 24-page *Dads University Trax Team Captain's Guide,* available for $3.50 from Family University, offers numerous suggestions for

launching and sustaining small fathering groups, curriculum suggestions, and a great selection of ice-breaker questions and activities.
(See the Dads University notice on page 190 to order).

Other Players in Your Child's Life

As great a father as you might be, your child will not be raised
by you alone—and that is fortunate. Gone are "Little House on the
Prairie" days, when a father had supreme control over everyone
who came in contact with his children. Today your child is probably under the care of others, whether in day-care or school. She is
influenced by radio, television, music, newspapers, videos, and
movies. As he grows older, he will spend increasing amounts of time
at work, on sports teams, in social organizations, and with friends.

So part of your job as a committed father is monitoring the
impact these other players make in your child's life—and making
the most of their involvement. Teachers, counselors, youth leaders,
coaches, and neighbors can make a big contribution. They parent
your kids when you aren't around. Expressing appreciation to these
adults only enhances their attitude toward your child. Esteem them
and their efforts in your child's behalf. Encourage them by volun-
teering in your child's classroom, by chaperoning field trips or par-
ties; by so doing you inspire them to keep up the good work and
increase their level of connection with your child.

Other significant adults in your child's life give you a fresh perspective of your child. For instance, talk to your daughter's teacher
to find out how she relates to a group. Talk to your son's employer
to discover what life skills and principles he's good at or how you
need to help him develop. Talk to your child's friends to see what
kinds of kids he associates with. These interactions yield a wealth
of information you can use to understand your child and learn how
best to father him.

Unfortunately, you must also protect your children from people
who can hurt them. Educate each child about appropriate and inappropriate behavior by other adults. Be
aware of who your child hangs out with,
and limit the contact if it is in the best
interest of the child. Equip your children
in advance for circumstances they will
encounter.

Think ahead. You can't keep your children sheltered their entire lives from out-

Smart Idea:
Secretly tape record your
family's breakfast-table
conversation next Saturday
or Sunday morning. Then
play it back that night as
a dinner surprise.

side influences, but you can stay ahead of the game by anticipating influences they will encounter and by going on the offensive.

Using Outside Resources

Although I believe every father can be strengthened by the insight and instruction he can gain from outside resources, some men are too busy, they don't tend to read about fathering and family issues, or they simply don't feel the need to look outside their own intuition or family circle for help.

Aerobics guru Dr. Kenneth Cooper admitted how difficult it was for him to accept the fact that he needed help from an outside resource for his then-young daughter, who had a learning disability that made learning to read very difficult. Cooper's first response was to tutor her himself. Many hours of trying to teach his daughter to read only frustrated him and discouraged his daughter.

Then he used his network. He contacted reading specialists and educators experienced in teaching children with his daughter's learning difficulty. Shedding that job was the best thing to do as a father, under the circumstances. The professionals succeeded at teaching his daughter to read. Cooper's willingness to use outside resources empowered his daughter to learn and greatly enhanced her self-esteem.

Many excellent fathering resources are available—books, tapes, videos, seminars, classes. Family University recommends these:

• **_Smart Dads._** A bimonthly subscription newsletter with a wealth of practical tips, ideas, and insights for fathering toddlers through teenagers. Published six times a year. Each year's subscription includes two semi-annual "Dad Talk" audio cassettes. (See page 190 for subscription information.)

• **Dads University.** A curriculum of half-day fathering courses that can be hosted in your city by community groups, churches, or corporations. Each course is taught by a trained and certified Family University instructor.

• **_Dad Trax._** A series of hour-long audio cassettes for drive-time listening, featuring a Reader's Digest-style potpourri

Smart Idea:
The "pits" is what exhausted parents call that last hour before dinner with tired, hungry, fussy kids. If you're not fixing the meal, scoop up the kids for a thirty-minute walk around the block, or clean out a closet or a toy box, or otherwise occupy everybody until the meal is ready.

of five-minute discussions on topics of interest to every dad (published by Family University).

• ***40 Ways to Teach Your Child Values***. A practical handbook of ideas for communicating forty important skills, attitudes, and values to children, from toddlers to teens.

• ***Famous Fathers***. A two-hour series of four videos featuring fathering stories, comments, and insights from celebrity fathers Stan Smith, Rosey Grier, Bill Gaither, Josh McDowell, Kenneth Cooper, and Noel Paul Stookey.

Other sources of excellent fathering resources are Focus on the Family (8665 Explorer Dr., Colorado Springs, CO 80920, phone 719/531-3400) and the National Center for Fathering (10200 W. 75th, Ste. 267, Shawnee Mission, KS 66204, phone 913/384-4661).

For those who want to build a small fathering library of your own, I suggest the following books and tapes:

• *The Seven Habits of Highly Successful Fathers*, Ken Canfield

• *Missing from Action: Vanishing Manhood in America*, Weldon Hardenbrook

• *Raising Self-Reliant Children in a Self-Indulgent World*, H. Stephen Glenn and Jane Nelson

• *The On My Own Handbook*, Bob Biehl

• *Tender Warrior: God's Intention for a Man*, Stu Weber

• *Fathers and Sons: The Wound, the Bond, and the Healing*, Gordon Dalby

• *Finding Our Fathers: How a Man's Life Is Shaped by His Relationship with His Father*, Sam Osherson

Worthy additions to this list appear regularly. You are invited to write to Family University for additional recommendations.

Habit Four: Communicating Life Skills and Principles

The Tire

In a Dads University course, I often ask men to form groups of three or four to introduce themselves to each other—but in this way: Each man is to assume the character of his own father, and introduce his son—that is, himself. (Phil, role-playing his father, says, "I'd like to introduce you to my son, Phil . . .")

The introductions are always animated and broken by laughter one minute, tears the next. Within the first few sentences, most men stop talking *as* their dads and revert to talking *about* their dads—in particular, the skills, lessons, and insights their dads taught them.

A man gets a special sparkle in his eye and pride in his voice when he says, "My dad taught me that—." I overheard my own sons say it recently to some neighborhood friends as they sawed wood and pounded nails on the patio, building something at the workbenches I made for them last Christmas.

As the project progressed, one of the playmates asked my boys more than once, "Hey, how'd you learn how to do that?"

"My dad taught me."

It felt good hearing that. I want to be my boys' primary instructor. I want to keep a clear channel of communication so they'll always know they can ask Dad, and that I'll give every answer my best shot— even if I have to respond, "I don't know, but I'll help you find out."

The fourth key habit of smart dads is that of giving your children a working understanding of the life skills and principles they will need to function successfully as adults.

In our wheel paradigm, this is the tire. Tires come in a great variety of styles and constructions, each suited to handle different weather and road conditions. We select tires with an eye to the roads we travel, the weather and driving conditions we anticipate. The ideal tire is strong and fairly adaptable to most road surfaces.

Five Key Habits of Smart Dads
FATHERING PARADIGM

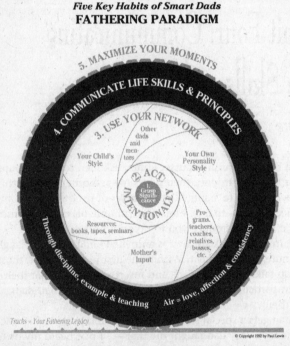

Start with a broad-based approach to communicating life skills and principles to your children. You see the world in which they live, the dilemmas they will face. Your assignment is to shape in your child the necessary character and commitments to safely maneuver through whatever challenges you can anticipate for them.

Today's rate of technological and cultural change is dizzying. But then, most generations feel that life moves faster for them than it did for their forbears. I ran across a small fathering book entitled *Dad, Whose Boy Is Yours?* The preface began, "The speed of modern living is terrific. Never before have there been so many demands upon each ten minutes of a man's time." I checked the copyright page and saw the date—1936.

The sense that modern life is rushing by isn't new, but the rate of change has seemed to accelerate, even by objective standards. One of my fathering concerns is to assess what skills my kids will need when, in a few years, they are on their own in an even more hyper world. How can I prepare them to live maturely in the very different world that ours will be twenty years from now?

The answer is to focus on principles and fundamentals. I must teach them a process for aiming at good answers, rather than giving them answers myself. I must teach them to assimilate timeless principles that ought to govern all decisions, regardless of cultural changes—truth, fairness, love, integrity, loyalty. I must teach them to accept responsibility for their own lives, to practice self-control, to express their feelings without hurting others in the process, to respond to others' needs.

I must help them recognize that, in their power of choice, they control much of their own destiny. I must introduce them to God, who holds their destiny in his hand, teaching them to love and obey him. (Later I will explain the connection I see between my relationship with God and how I relate to my children as a father.)

Teach Them How to Think

Ask questions.

Teaching your child *how* to think and reason is infinitely better than teaching them *what* to think.

Asking questions is the chief way of teaching children how to think. Say you are teaching your son to wait his turn in line. One Saturday morning at the playground you notice him cut in front of other kids. You could say, "Hey, I told you to wait your turn." Or you could ask him, "What have I taught you about taking turns when using the slide?" The question

Smart Idea:
Kidnap your child for lunch this week. Find out the exact time school breaks for lunch, notify the school office, and show up outside the classroom door. A nearby fast-food restaurant will do the trick. When it's your *wife* you kidnap for lunch, take her to a restaurant at the mall.

requires him to find his own answer—based on your instruction—
and apply it. Your next question might be about how he should correct his behavior or repair the feelings of others.

It can be a bit trickier with older children, especially when
moral issues are involved, but the approach is the same—*what*
questions rather than *why* questions yield far better results in terms
of shaping character and sponsoring maturity:

• "What is wrong with driving home from a party after you
have taken a drink?"

• "What consequence did we agree you would experience?"

• "What are you risking when you choose to cheat on a test?"
(or "to lie to me" or "to be sexually active")

• "What will it take to reestablish trust between us?"

Let them choose between good options.

Hone decision-making skills in younger children by giving them
options. Once your daughter can talk, ask her, "Do you want to wear
your blue dress or your green one?" "Do you want to have an egg or
pancakes?" When she grows older and contemplates a poor choice,
you can set firm limitations, yet at the same time offer options.

Your teenage girl wants to date too soon, for instance. You can
set firm limits with "No, you can't date until you're sixteen." But
don't stop there—give her some options: "You can have a boy you
want to know better visit with our family at home or go out to dinner with us." This way she can practice making appropriate decisions, though within your limits.

It is essential that rules of behavior in your family are clear and
clearly communicated. It's even better when a fair and clear penalty
for breaking the rule is attached to each. If established up front,
before the infraction occurs, you have the luxury of responding in
sympathy with your child in terms of the discipline to be dished
out, rather than being in the position of playing judge and jury,
making up the penalty on the spot. Post the basic rules you agree
on in a conspicuous spot.

Some examples of what family rules might be:

• Courtesies—if you open it, close it. If you turn it on, turn
it off. If you break it, repair it. If you can't repair it, report
it. If you use it, don't abuse it. If you make a mess, clean it
up. If you move it, put it back.

• Personal stuff is private. Get permission first.

- Homework and chores precede TV and video games.
- Truth rules—we never lie to each other.
- If you won't be home on time, call.
- If your plans change midstream, report them first.
- Family plans and commitments come first.

If you and your spouse don't agree on a particular rule, work out a compromise. A lack of clarity here sends very confusing messages to your children.

Let them tell you why.

Once you establish rules and principles that guide your family, ask questions to help your child think through the reasoning behind your rules. When a child protests "Why can't I?" to a limiting rule you lay down, you can ask, "You tell me: Why can't you do that? Why is this important?" Thinking about reasons behind rules does not spawn little rebels, but cultivates healthy, active consciences.

Help them find their own answers.

Don't give your children all the answers. Help them instead to learn the process for finding answers. My daughter Shelley often asks me to spell a word for her. If I'm busy, I'm tempted to simply spell the word for her. But I do better when I say, "Try it yourself, Shelley, while I listen." Eight times out of ten times she spells it right, and trying it builds her confidence.

If a child has a school project due, go to the library and show her how to find the information she needs. Lead her in trying various paths to follow in obtaining her research . . . in projecting what will likely result from each of the routes she proposes. Suggest whom she could ask for help when she exhausts her own ideas. This kind of teaching does more good than merely giving answers to a child's questions.

In short, ask questions whenever your child—

- Needs to stop and think about his behavior.
- Needs reminding about a rule being broken.

Smart Idea:
Spring these riddles on your kids:
- What is everybody in the world doing at the same time? (Growing older)
- What is the center of gravity? (The letter V)
- What word is always pronounced wrong? (Wrong)
- What can go up the chimney down, but can't go down the chimney up? (An umbrella)

- **Needs to think about the rights or feelings of others.**
- **Needs encouragement to make the right moral choice.**

How you ask questions is important, too:

- **Lower your voice and avoid sarcasm.**
- **Ask only one question at a time.**
- **Use questions to keep your emotions under control.**
- **Repeat your question if your child is avoiding the right answer.**
- **Use questions instead of statements to remind the child of what he already has been taught. ("What have I told you about waiting in line?")**

The Importance of How You Communicate

Strong families communicate with each other clearly and regularly. Communication is a set of skills you can develop. You're certainly at an advantage if you came from a family that communicated well; but even if communication was poor in your home, you can learn what makes for successful communication and practice these skills as you interact with your children.

Communicate with a spirit of love.

The tire represents the important life skills and principles your child needs to acquire. Just as the best tire in the world won't take you far if it's flat, so you must inflate the life skills and principles you communicate with the air of your love, affection, and consistency—the fatherly combination that allows this tire to roll. If you try to communicate even the right things, but without a spirit of love, your attempt will be futile.

This point is made eloquently in the New Testament by the Apostle Paul:

> If I speak in the tongues of men and of angels, but have not love, I am only a resounding gong or a clanging cymbal. If I have the gift of prophecy and can fathom all mysteries and all knowledge, and if I have a faith that can move mountains, but have not love, I am nothing. If I give all I possess to the poor and surrender my body to the flames, but have not love, I gain nothing. (1 Cor. 13:1-3)

It's difficult for some men to actively love their children because love, they believe wrongly, is a feeling (although it is true that when you love your children, you will likely generate loving feelings). Love is a verb, not a noun. Love is action. Love is choosing to do whatever is necessary for the well-being of your children. As you love your children, they will become receptive to whatever you communicate to them—including life skills and principles. Yet the most correct instruction in the world won't make much difference in your children if at the same time you do not demonstrate your active love for them.

Demonstrate your love by telling your children how much you love them, listening intently when they talk, showing physical affection (hugs, kisses, wrestling, an arm around the shoulder, a pat on the head), spending time with them, paying attention to them, speaking to them respectfully, and faithfully caring for their needs.

Communicating with a spirit of love means that you—

• **Talk directly to one another.** If you have something to say to your wife or daughter, go to her directly instead of talking about her to other members of the family. Don't rely on them overhearing a comment made about them to provoke them to respond. Couriers of your message will only distort it—plus you'll probably hurt the feelings of the person talked about, or you'll betray a confidence.

• **Don't rely on rumors.** Go to the source. Make sure that what you heard *about* someone is in truth what was actually said or done.

• **Listen very carefully.** Listening deeply shows respect for your children and earns their respect. When a child tries to talk to you, exercise enough patience to let him say what he's trying to say rather than finishing the sentence for him. Take time to listen. Give the child feedback to make sure you understand her—then make sure she knows that you did actually hear her.

• **Keep your conflicts out in the open.** Strong families have fights and get mad at each other, but they keep their conflicts out in the open. They honestly discuss differences and aren't passive-aggressive in punishing each other (like giving someone the silent treatment).

• **Work toward resolution.** Remain committed to talking through a disputed issue until a solution is reached that is best for everybody.

Build communication bridges by blessing your child.

If you want to get across to your children the life skills and principles you have to communicate, actively and regularly bless your child. Authors Gary Smalley

Smart Idea:
A person's last thoughts of the day remain in the subconscious all night. It's a good reason, as you say goodnight to your child, to praise her for a character strength you admire or an act or word of hers that made you proud of her.

and John Trent offer this excellent formula for conveying a strong sense of your blessing:

• **Meaningful touch.** Make a habit of touching your child in positive ways. A hug, kiss, or a pat on the back makes your words real to them. Children need lots of meaningful touch; research shows that it actually causes positive physiological changes when you touch your child with affection.

• **Spoken words.** Say what you mean. Say what you feel toward your child. Spoken words, words of instruction, praise, affirmation, are all powerful ways to convey love.

Solomon, acknowledged in the ancient world as enormously wise, wrote that "death and life are in the power of the tongue" (Prov. 18:21). Accordingly, when you say, "Jason, the way you stood up for your sister today makes me proud. That took real courage," you affirm not only the act, but also the value of the child. What commonly keeps fathers from verbally blessing their children are workaholism, withdrawal, simple procrastination, or the fact that they were never blessed verbally by their own father.

• **Express the high value you place on your child.** Tell your child often how much you value him or her. Comment on specific character traits and physical attributes that you admire and appreciate. Let your son know that you like the way he dressed and groomed himself. Express your appreciation for the way your daughter comes home every day and does her homework without being told to do so.

• **Picture a special future.** Envision the best happening in your child's life and express that vision ("Boy, with a pitching arm like that you could be in the major leagues").

• **Be actively committed to helping your child succeed.** When you communicate important life skills, take steps to equip the child to experience success with the skill you are teaching. When you teach your young son how to groom himself properly, for instance, it's not enough to tell him to take a shower and wash his hair if he has never been *taught* to shower and shampoo on his own. So teach him how— and remember that teaching includes helping him overcome any fear he has of the water or of getting shampoo in his eyes, it includes using nonirritating shampoo to *guarantee* his eyes won't burn, giving him the brushes to do his own hair, and so on.[1]

Let your children learn from your experience.

Your children learn how life works when you share your life with them. So let your kids learn from both your successes and your failures. Give them a taste of the struggles you face outside your home. Men tend not to talk about their problems and insecurities with their families, perhaps because we fear we will appear weak or because we want to shelter our family from worry. But when your children see that you're not perfect, then they can more easily share *their* problems and insecurities.

So model not only your virtues, but model also your frankness about your faults. Kids don't expect perfection in you, but they will profit from your doing your best to live true to your own values. Teach them the importance of honesty by acting honestly. Teach them the importance of wearing seat belts by buckling up. Live the values you want your child to learn.

"He was my teacher," Kevin Costner said of his father, "and he taught me about loyalty and friendship and doing your best. . . . Truth and those things are never far out of style."[2]

Demonstrate the skills you want to teach them.

Before expecting your child to do something properly, you must instruct him adequately and thoroughly. You cannot simply assign a young child a new chore, expect it to be completed, and then—when the child inevitably fails at it—deflate her with "If I want something done right around here, I have to do it myself."

Overcome your impatience by working in pairs at a skill. It promotes cooperation, respect, mutual support, and makes large jobs easier. When the pair is a parent and child, furthermore, you have a natural reason to be together and talk—plus your quality-control may be less threatening.

Another way to demonstrate skills you want your child to learn is to take him with you to your workplace and show him what you do there. Not too many generations ago, children saw the work their fathers did; many, in fact, learned trades at the hands of their fathers.

These days, though "work" steals fathers from their children, few children have a clue about what their fathers do at work all day. Yet on occasion—and depending on the ages of your children and the nature of your work—you can take your child to work or on a business trip. (One dad I know takes each child along with him every year on a business

> **Smart Idea:**
> As you're tucking your child into bed, get crazy. "Hey, let's camp out in the living room tonight!" Grab two sleeping bags and a flashlight. Make shadow animals on the ceiling, talk about your day, and plan a real campout together in the near future.

trip.) If your children are self-disciplined enough and your work is conducive to having them present, these are excellent times to spend with your child, to communicate how important the child is to you, and to help her understand your job and the realities you contend with.

These reminders have helped me when I plan a business trip with my children:

- **Spell out the ground rules.**
- **If she will miss school, arrange for her to bring homework along to fill up the time when you are busy.**
- **Plan time to visit a historical site or take in a fun activity unique to your destination.**

Release children progressively throughout life.

Practice equipping and releasing your child. From childhood onward, give them freedom and confidence in their own abilities.

It's like teaching him to ride a bicycle. First he graduates from the tricycle. Then he learns to maneuver a two-wheeler with training wheels. When you see he's got the idea, you take off the training wheels—but you still don't just let him go. You hold on, running alongside; as long as he stays up, you keep your hands off the bike (but never far from it). When he wobbles, you catch him. You keep encouraging, coaching, and letting go until he can keep his balance indefinitely and no longer needs you running alongside. What you've done is give him freedom and confidence in his own ability.

Letting go is a process that you need to practice from day one with your children. If they are taught to accept responsibility for their own lives, then step by step we end up with grown children who can cope with life successfully when they leave our care. If we still have to remind our children to do their homework, pick up their clothes, and be home on time well past the age when they should be responsible for these tasks on their own, they will not be prepared to deal successfully with life on their own, when we're not around.

It is during the early years of childhood that these skills are most effectively taught, with only touch-up and fine-tuning during junior high and high school. If you can do this, your children will learn how to monitor themselves and make good choices in most circumstances. A child that comes of age functionally unable to care for himself, on the other hand, will not thank you for your concern and care over the years, but will likely resent you—even blame you when he is unprepared to bear the sudden pressures of responsible adulthood.

Let young children learn from experience.

We need to reverse parents' tendency to overprotect young children and underprotect their teens. Your young children are probably already fairly well protected. Within the controlled, safe environment of your home and under your watchful eye, you can afford to allow your youngsters to feel the relatively minor consequences of their disobedience or poor choices. They can afford to skin their knees a few times or get physically rebuffed if they get aggressive with another child. Your child learns how the world really works by experiencing consequences of his behavior. She gains a rock-solid understanding of what it means to reap what she sows.

Protecting young children from the consequences of their actions fosters unrealistic expectations. They tend to enter the outside world thinking that they can do whatever they want, and expect someone to step in and protect them from the consequences. The evidence is all around us that that is exactly how too many teenagers were raised: widespread experimentation with dangerous drugs, dangerous driving habits, recreational sex—a general avoidance of responsibility for their actions. It is during your child's preadolescent and adolescent season that you must be *more* vigilant in monitoring behaviors with life-threatening consequences.

Monitor teenage children with vigilance.

Teenagers believe they are immortal. They know all the facts about AIDS, drinking and driving, and drug addiction—and assume that bad things happen only to others, never to them. So it is up to you to protect your teenager from whatever behaviors that have perilous, lifelong consequences. Emerging adults gain courage to act responsibly from the strength of the father-child connection—more, in fact, than from the mother-child connection. During this phase parents need to be especially vigilant.

Discipline.

Effective discipline is another powerful way fathers instill in their children the life skills and principles that lead to success. Discipline teaches your children the reali-

> **Smart Thought:**
> Hugs are therapeutic. Would your family become better at expressing love if each member made a point of hugging the others at least once a day? And don't let a week go by without a "family hug."

ties of life's proper boundaries and the self-control to live happily within them.

You've watched it happen often. Young children throw a temper tantrum when told they can't have the cookie or toy. They may lash out at you physically or verbally. An appropriate spanking or canceling a cherished privilege for "acting that way" is an entirely suitable response, as long as you also explain what kinds of negotiations with you are acceptable alternatives.

Children who learn how to control their temper and mouths early in their lives will be way ahead when they become adolescents—and so will you. You'll have teenagers whose first reaction to being denied a request isn't to sneak around you or storm out of the house or abuse you verbally, but to respectfully negotiate with you for the freedoms they want.

Yet each of your children is different, and each responds differently to different kinds of discipline. So study your children for what kind of discipline each child responds to most. One child toes the line if he so much as notices your eyebrow go up at the mere suspicion of a stretched household rule. His sister, on the other hand, may need extended "time outs" to think about her misbehavior. Keep each child's unique nature in mind as you try to achieve balance and fairness in establishing consequences for wrong behavior. Tailor the punishment to the temperament of your child.

As often as possible, set up disciplinary measures (or consequences) in advance of infractions. This helps your children to envision the impact of a bad choice and to take ownership of the outcome. If children can predict the disciplinary measures, then choose their behavior accordingly, you've given them a skill that will navigate them around all manner of bad consequences throughout life. If you bail them out too often, you diminish what they need to learn from the experience.

Here are some discipline guidelines:

- **Adapt your discipline to what works with each child.**
- **Set clear standards for appropriate and inappropriate behavior.**
- **Make sure each child understands your standards.**
- **Decide the penalty for violating a particular behavior before that behavior occurs.**
- **Make sure the penalties are consistently enforced from infraction to infraction and from child to child.**

- As much as possible, allow the penalty to be associated with the natural consequences of poor choices.

Teaching children to get along with others.

In families children learn foundational skills for getting along with others. Plan ways to make the most of the quarrels that inevitably occur. Help your children come up with successful ways to work together, solve their problems, work through differing opinions, and settle disputes. Children need to learn how to negotiate a positive solution—and they gain that skill as you require them to experiment and practice working out the differences between them.

For example, the next time your two children (who are developmentally able to carry out this assignment) are caught quarreling, try this: Send each to a different corner of the room, but sitting so that they face each other. Tell them they must remain there until each is ready to make peace with the other. The resulting negotiations usually quickly lead to peace again. In the process, you have helped your children learn to resolve conflicts through cooperation.

Conduct family councils often, for they lead to fair solutions for problems between members and encourage family participation in rule making and problem solving. Draw up a list of family-council procedures that all agree to. Your list may look like this:

- **Anyone can tell parents how he or she feels, and ask for a meeting.**
- **At the meeting, everyone can say what he or she thinks about a situation.**
- **Instead of fixing blame, the council must try to understand why there's a problem.**
- **The council will try to create a solution that's fair to all.**

Role playing is another tool for sharpening confrontation and problem-solving skills. It's a creative communication tool that promotes listening, empathy, and new patterns for managing conflict.

Here's how to do it: Describe an actual problem among some members of your family. Recreate the incident, though with switched characters—that is, with various members of your family putting themselves in another person's position. Replay

Smart Idea:
Shake up your mealtime routine by staging an old-fashioned progressive dinner—all at your house. Appetizer in a bedroom, vegetable or salad in the family room, main course in another bedroom, and dessert in the garage or basement.

the situation, experimenting with alternate responses and reactions. Then, over a bowl of popcorn, talk about how each of you felt in the various roles and what was learned from the experience that could help solve the problem.

Role play is also an excellent way to let your children rehearse good decisions (about issues they'll face in the near future) and the words that explain or defend those decisions. At many points, for instance, your child will encounter tough, persistent, negative peer pressure. So role-play situations in which peers try to get your son to do something he shouldn't do. Rehearsing can be good preparation; he can try on comfortable ways to say no without looking foolish. It could spell the difference between being lured into dangerous behavior and having the self-confidence to resist.

Keeping communication lines open.

It's far easier to keep communication lines open than to repair them once they're broken.

I used to do something I called "Monday Night Interviews" with my kids. Every Monday evening after dinner, I spent twenty minutes with cassette recorder in hand, asking each child questions about what happened during the weekend, during that day at school, and what each child expects to do the rest of the week. Any question was fair game; I tended to focus on their friends, pets, hobbies, and achievements.

Or turn the tables and let your children interview *you*. Or play a light-hearted game of "Truth or Dare," in which each takes turns asking questions that must be answered truthfully. The person who is asked the question can then choose to answer or do something silly that the questioner dares them to do.

Another simple communication builder: Give each child the chance to stay up with you an extra thirty or sixty minutes once a week. Younger children especially relish the chance to stay up past their normal bedtime. Spend the time lying on your backs, talking about the family, the kind of day the child has had, or planning a future adventure. The lost sleep is insignificant compared to the relationship you're strengthening.

Before they leave home.

I aim to communicate the life skills and principles I want each child to know by their junior year in high school. This way I have their senior year to watch how well they've got a grip on these skills and make necessary corrections. Setting this deadline forces me to decide specifically what I want to communicate, what skills I want them to be proficient at, what values and attitudes I want to see ingrained in their character. Let these ideas get you started:

Skills

- Handling finances responsibly
- Balancing a checkbook
- Decision making
- How to make, keep, and treat friends
- Coping with guilt
- Accepting criticism and correction
- Dealing with death
- Personal grooming and cleanliness
- Home management skills
- Spiritual life habits and disciplines

Attitudes

- A can-do spirit
- Kicking the blues
- Turning negatives into positives
- Looking on the bright side
- A sense of humor
- Persevering and acting with diligence
- Appreciation of simplicity
- Counting their blessings
- Self-respect
- Servanthood

Values

- Honesty
- Personal integrity
- Taming TV
- Family traditions
- Respect for others' privacy
- Appropriate modesty
- The value of hard work
- Appreciation for the arts
- A love of learning
- Courage

Smart Idea:
"I thought of you when I saw this!" are magic words when scrawled on a note and taped to something—flower, picture, magazine clipping, travel brochure, candy—that you leave out for your child or wife to discover.

When your quarterly father review and evaluation rolls around, use some of your time to chart where each child is in his or her progress toward learning the life skills and principles you want them to learn.

Imagine a scale from one (poor) to ten (excellent) next to each of the above skills, attitudes, and values; now mentally rate their competency. Keep your expectations reasonable, considering the age and development of each child. Then let this evaluation you've compiled guide you into the next quarter as you decide where in particular to help and encourage them.

Celebrate Rites of Passage

Many cultures celebrate rites of passage—positive steps toward adulthood that are celebrated and recognized by society to help children make the transition from childhood to adulthood. In Jewish culture it is the bar (or bat) mitzvah, in which the community comes together to celebrate a young person becoming responsible before God for his or her own life.

In modern American culture, however, rites of passage are virtually nonexistent. Yet just because you raise your children in a culture that doesn't celebrate rites of passage doesn't mean that you can't at least create some markers for your children.

A wise father thinks through important milestones in life, helping his children chart and celebrate their progress. When *you* treat such milestones importantly, your children will similarly attach value to their progress.

The onset of puberty is a key marker in your child's development. I celebrate this rite of passage on each child's thirteenth birthday. I start by writing a letter, acknowledging her uniqueness— what I respect and honor about her life. I affirm him in as many specific ways as I can. In the letter I recognize and honor personal strengths. Writing this letter is a way to express my appreciation of her, to describe him in writing, to recognize his idiosyncrasies I want to applaud.

Over dinner at a special restaurant (of her choice), I read the letter to her. I listen to whatever reponse she has to the letter. We discuss the transition to becoming a young

Smart Idea:

These days it's hard to keep extended families in touch.

Create an address list of relatives and initiate a round-robin letter. Mail your short family update and a couple of photos to the next address, along with instructions for them to do the same for the next family, and so forth.

woman and the new responsibilities she will soon assume. I recognize that he will want more freedoms, which I tell him I will gladly give— but in exchange for the greater responsibilities that go with them.

I acknowledge her passage into the zone of premarital sexual control. Controlling one's sexuality is a mark of maturity and of one's sense of well-being. I admit to her that many are sexually irresponsible, but I stress the benefits of self-control, of waiting for sex within marriage. I help her see the beauty of genuine sexuality in contrast to the devalued sexual mores in our culture. I express clearly my expectations as her dad.

This may sound heavy, but it's really a festive time of looking both backward and forward. We celebrate the other few rites of passage that are significant in our culture—getting a driver's license, getting their first job, using the family car, graduation, and so on. These are prime moments to talk about increasing responsibility and to reinforce new life skills and principles needed to successfully make the transition.

Have in Mind a Clear Picture of Success

The very helpful book *Raising Self-Reliant Kids in a Self-Indulgent World* lists seven foundational capabilities of successful young people—skills and perceptions found in children who have the ability to consistently make mature choices. According to authors H. Stephen Glenn and Jane Nelson, successful kids will have—

- **The perception that they are significant.**
- **The perception that they are capable.**
- **The perception that they have potent control over their environment.**
- **The skill of understanding themselves.**
- **The skill of understanding others.**
- **The skill to flex and adapt.**
- **The skill to make effective judgments.**

Regularly picture in your mind your child's success and his next stages of development, and then make the most of each opportunity to help your child grow—every day, every week.

A final note about communicating life skills and principles to your children: It is never too late for a father to start doing what is right. Communicating life skills and principles is no exception. Only recognize that it gets proportionately more difficult the later in your child's life you start. So take action today to make the most of the time and opportunity you now have.

9

Habit Five:
Maximizing Your Moments
The Tread

I always kissed my father goodnight and we always enjoyed a certain warmth, but we never talked seriously. We were from two different planets. He died in 1964 at age 55 when I was fourteen years old. I felt then, as I do now: that he had labored tirelessly to "get ahead" at the price of never having been able to stop and try to know what it or we were all about. His was a selfless labor for kids he barely had time to know.[1]

—JOE RUSSO,
PARTICIPANT AT MULTICULTURAL MEN'S STUDIES SEMINAR

I don't want my children to write about me like this.

In our fathering paradigm the tread on the tire represents maximizing your moments with your children. Each of those nubs, bumps, and contours represent an incident, a conversation, a Saturday morning at the baseball field or on the lake, an errand a few blocks away, a vacation, angry or loving words of discipline or correction—any of a million possibilities, but each one a moment of relationship and interchange between your child and you.

Five Key Habits of Smart Dads
FATHERING PARADIGM

5. MAXIMIZE YOUR MOMENTS

4. COMMUNICATE LIFE SKILLS & PRINCIPLES

3. USE YOUR NETWORK

Your Child's Style

Other dads and mentors

Your Own Personality Style

2. ACT INTENTIONALLY

1. Grasp Significance

Resources: books, tapes, seminars

Programs, teachers, coaches, relatives, bosses, etc.

Mother's Input

Through discipline, example & teaching   Air = love, affection & consistency

Tracks = Your Fathering Legacy

© Copyright 1992 by Paul Lewis

Added together these moments form a noticeable, unique pattern. As a tire's tread leaves an imprint, the time you spend with your children shapes the imprint of your life on theirs. Moments grand and small, magical and mundane—these are the stuff of which memories are made.

How and where you spend your discretionary moments tells the tale. You can use your moments to know your children, to express your love for them, to teach and guide them, to let them know you—or you can invest your moments in other responsibilities, as Joe Russo's father apparently did.

Give your children time to know you. Take lots of pictures and videos, take time to write notes and letters, make audio recordings of your thoughts or of reading stories to your children. Compile a scrapbook of clippings you find that reflect ideas and values that drive your life. Create lots of physical evidence of you, for someday it will be treasured by your children and grandchildren—just as you treasure anything you may have of your grandparents.

Two summers ago Leslie and I celebrated our twenty-fifth anniversary with a visit to Great Britain—and took along my father and mother to celebrate their *fiftieth*. I especially looked forward to spending a day or two in Breckon County, in the south of Wales, from which my great-great-great-grandfather emigrated to the United States.

We called some relatives to learn what we could about my Welsh ancestor before we left on the trip. A cousin of my grandfather finally sent us details about our family tree, including the fact that in 1857 John Lewis—my great-great-great-grandfather—had married Ann Vaughn in Crickhowell, Wales.

Finally locating Crickhowell on a map, we set aside a day to drive there.

We spent a night at a bed-and-breakfast farmhouse in the village of Cum Dee, a short walk from the ruins of a Norman castle that had been partially restored by a Vaughn family. The relatives of Ann Vaughn, we wondered? In explaining our genealogical quest to our Cum Dee host the next morning, we learned that he and the head librarian in Breckon—the county seat fourteen miles away—were good friends.

With this referral we were ushered into the Breckon library, where a clerk set to work. The search eventually took us to the county records office looking for a public record of the marriage of John Lewis and Ann Vaughn. Two hours later on a call to the recorder in a nearby town, the voice on the other end of the line said, "Here it is." The other clerk had in hand a copy of John and Ann's marriage certificate, which named a farm not two miles from the bed and breakfast at which we had stayed.

A couple hours later my father and I pushed open a gate at the end of a narrow country lane and walked toward a weathered, grey stone farm house. The occupants were obviously sheepherders—in the middle of lambing season, at that, for ewes and new offspring were everywhere.

We knocked on the white picket gate, and out of the house came a small man in tattered clothing, though bright, clear eyes set in a sun-weathered face. Dad unfolded the paper on which was outlined John Lewis's branch of our family tree, and handed it to the shepherd with an explanation of who we were and what we wanted ed. The little man studied it for a minute;

Smart Idea:
Young children can create wonderful stories. Take dictation from your child, then read the story back to him. Keep his stories in a special notebook; they make great reading years later, too.

then, exhorting us not to leave yet, he turned and walked back into the house.

When he returned a few moments later, he held an aged family Bible—six inches thick with deeply embossed covers and brass latches on the side. He opened it to the middle, and there on the family record pages, laid out line by line, was the Lewis family tree.

This sheep farmer turned out to be a distant relative of ours with a keen interest in genealogy. He led us into his small kitchen to show us a keepsake—a tall, plain grandfather clock ticking away up against the wall. This, he explained, was the wedding present John Lewis gave Ann Vaughn. (We got it all on video.)

It was difficult to believe that I was standing in the kitchen of my great-great-great-grandfather, running my hand along the woodwork of a clock he had undoubtedly wound hundreds of times. How I wanted to talk with John Lewis for just a day or two—the John Lewis who loved and married a woman named Ann, who began a family before bringing them all to America.

As it is, apart from a handful of details, John Lewis is only a name to me. The rest I must guess at. What I wouldn't give for a recording of his voice and laughter, a journal of his thoughts, even a clear photo. I wondered about the relatives whose names were listed in the sheep farmer's Bible—much like a man's own children and grandchildren will wonder about a father who does not give enough of his time to his children so that he is known deeply by them.

Children Spell Love T-I-M-E

Your time is the currency your children will value most. Gifts of your presence mean more than any presents you may give. Children understand that time is valuable; so when we have inadequate time for our children, they eventually interpret this to mean that we don't value them.

Quality Time, or Quantity of Time?

How much time does a good father spend with his child? That's a hard question to answer; most fathers I talk to say they don't feel they have enough time with their children. Only you can gauge the substance of the minutes and hours you invest in your fathering legacy.

Smart Idea:
Ask you wife to list five things she wants done around the house during the next month—then surprise her by getting all five done.

Without a doubt, however, any relationship requires time to grow and blossom. It is not enough to say your *life* is committed to your children if you have not committed substantial *time* to be with them. While you can usually add more quality to the time you spend with your children, the quality will always be in direct proportion to the quantity of time.

Time with your kids—and lots of it—is important because teachable moments almost always crop up at odd and unpredictable times. The more you are with your child, then, the greater the odds you'll be there when a teachable moment arrives.

Several years ago when my now-married daughter was in junior high, I listed the family vacation experiences I wanted to share with her before she left for college and wouldn't be home during the summers. I was stunned when I realized I was already two summers short to complete my list.

That got my attention. Although you and I get eighteen or so years with our kids, those years do not stretch on endlessly. I have only a window of time with each child. I began to deliberately look for and guard the times, large and small, I could spend with her.

No Quality
without Emotional Energy

There is scant quality in the time you spend with your children if you drag in the door most evenings, emotionally drained. It's a start at better fathering to get home at a respectable hour. But if the anxieties of your job follow you in the door, the quality of your time with your family plummets. A father must manage his emotional reserves just as he does his time reserves. His family deserves and needs more than emotional leftovers.

It doesn't get easier, either. Older children and teenagers are experts at sensing just how interested you are in what they're telling you when you interact with them. If you're emotionally wrung out, you cannot give and take in your family relationships the way your family needs you to relate. Learn to ration your emotional energy for home as you probably learned to do for work, so that you are prepared to be emotionally present with your wife and children.

Plan to Play

Play is a prime moment maximizer—not to mention a great stress reducer. Playing with your children reduces fathering guilt, helps you relax, restores your emotional energy—and makes your kids very happy.

If by *play* we mean any kind of pleasant interaction, think for a moment what it accomplishes with your child.

Play enhances self-esteem.

Play says, "I like you! You're important to me. You're fun!" Watch the eyes of your ten-year-old brighten when you say, "Hey Buddy—let's go play!" or watch your preschooler's sad expression when you brush off her request "Daddy, will you play with me?"

Play with me or trade me!

Used with permission of Hoest and *Ladies Home Journal*

Play builds bridges.

Whether it involves a sport, dolls, a hobby, or just unhurried, unguarded conversation, play builds bridges of mutual interest and experiences that last a lifetime. Aren't many of your fondest memories the spontaneous times of wrestling with your dad on the floor or just acting silly?

Play builds respect.

When you don't play with your kids, it's harder for them to obey you. Both discipline and intimate talk flow more naturally after playing together, because your child senses your loving heart in your play.

So give priority to playing with your kids. Start with ten minutes of tag before dinner, a bedtime chat over a bowl of popcorn, a joke at breakfast, a game of Chutes and Ladders or Candyland with your preschooler. Even cleaning the attic or washing the car make great play if you simply remain a kid at heart yourself.

Maximize Your Time with Kids

Besides play, here are some other ways to maximize the moments you have with your children.

Choose the right place.

Become aware of the settings in which your child seems to be most open to you.

In one father's master bedroom were two blue chairs, set facing each other. When a time came to talk deliberately to one of his children, he pulled his son or daughter into the bedroom and into those blue chairs. So many good conversations happened there, he began to notice that when one of the kids wanted to talk with him about something important to them, they'd ask, "Dad, can we go talk in the blue chairs?" To the children, the blue chairs were a safe place to communicate.

A mother of a couple teenagers noticed that they talked to her more openly when just the two of them, mother and child, were in the car. She didn't understand what the car had to do with it, but she made good use of the phenomenon anyway. Whenever her daughter or son seemed distant, she contrived a reason to drive them somewhere. And more often than not, once in the car they opened up and talked.

When my now-married daughter was a teenager, we lived in a mountain community an hour out of San Diego. We had horses, too, during that time, and plodding along dirt roads on horseback became an easy setting for conversations. In fact, my most significant conversations with her about sex were during those horseback rides.

Keep your antenna out for a place or setting in which your kids tend to open up—and then, whenever you sense your child wants or needs to talk, deliberately settle into those chairs or take a drive or saddle up.

Choose the right time.

Similarly, watch for those times when your child opens up to you. Some kids

> **Smart Idea:**
> Help shape your older child's growing independence by presenting on each birthday a roster of new privileges and responsibilities. Talk over last year's list and celebrate the areas of significant growth.

share more easily at bedtime, when they have quieted down after a busy day. Others are most receptive as soon as you get home, or on Saturday mornings. Notice the time of day interchange seems to flow easiest with your child—and do your best to be there then.

Be prepared to use stray moments.

You can do a lot of fathering during random moments here and there—ten minutes waiting for your wife to finish dressing . . . three minutes of commercials between TV action . . . ten minutes until the game or news comes on. A smart dad harnesses such moments.

Or try the "One-Minute Memo," a note of praise or love on a colored three-by-five card you keep handy for such impromptu - occasions. If you're stumped about what to write, start with these ideas:

- **Praise**—Write three sentences praising one of her qualities.
- **Specific thank-yous**—"Thank you, Casey, for helping me carry in the groceries without being asked. I really appreciate your help!"
- **Inspiration**—Write a favorite poem, a verse of Scripture, or a brief anecdote that reminded you of your child.
- **Catch-up note**—"I've been thinking of you a lot today, Jon. We haven't had much time together recently. How about going out for ice cream this weekend?"
- **Check up**—List jobs you want the child to do, with instructions to check them off when a task is completed and return the list to you—for a surprise reward.

My point is this: You *do* have time with your child, even if it is very little time. Make the most of what time you have with your children.

Maximize Your Moments *Away* from Your Children

Post-It notes.

Keep a pad of them in your desk or in your planner book exclusively for your children. When you think of things to tell them during your day, write them down in short notes: "You looked nice in your green sweater today". . . "Thanks for washing the car". . . "Let's go shopping for new tennis shoes tonight." Before you leave the house for work the next morning, leave these notes where your child will find them—the kitchen counter or their bathroom mirror, for example.

Don't leave unsaid those expressions of love you think of when you are away from them. Write 'em down and let your kids know that you think about them during your day.

When you're away from your toddlers overnight.

Before you leave, photocopy the pages of a couple short story-books. Take the copies with you. At bedtime call home and read the story over the phone while the child follows along in the book. The phone call may cost you more than the photocopies, but the investment pays big dividends in proving to your children that even when you are away from them, you reach out to them with love.

Smart dads who will be away for several nights may find it easier to record several bedtime stories on a cassette tape; Mom can play back your reading of a story at just the right moment with the book propped up in the child's lap. You can even use a whistle or finger snap to indicate when to turn the page.

And there's always the mail.

Before you leave, address and stamp several envelopes and a few postcards and tuck them into your briefcase. This makes it easy to dash off a quick note or enclose a cartoon or news clipping or anything else you noticed that reminded you of your child. Slip in a match book or other memento; if you brought a camera along, use a one-hour photo lab so you can enclose some snapshots of what you have been doing, seeing, or maybe the people with whom you're involved.

Checklist for traveling dads.

• Take a copy of your kid's schedule (including the phone number where she will spend the night on a sleepover, etc.).

• Take postcards, envelopes, stamps—whatever will help you write home frequently. Kids love mail—or a telegram if time is short (or if you'd beat a letter home).

• Leave behind a hidden surprise (pack of gum, a dollar for some ice cream, a brainteaser, etc.) that you can reveal when you're on the phone with your child.

• Plan a special moment to share together when you return home.

Smart Idea:
There's probably a magazine devoted specifically to your child's hobby or interest. Check the library for such lists of periodicals. Then give your child a personal subscription to the most suitable one—and read the issues together.

• Once in a while, surprise everyone by returning early. Get home the day before you said you would or six hours early. Scoop everyone up for an impromptu walk in the park or pizza dinner.

Essentials for long-distance dads.

No one denies how difficult it is to maintain a relationship with your children when you do not live with them—but it can be done. From the experience of fathers and the advice of professionals come several helpful reminders:

• Strive for consistency. Regular, small moments express love far better than infrequent "Disneyland" extravaganzas.

• Make and sustain contact with your child's school teachers. Knowing how they're doing in school will help you better support and encourage them. Direct contact with the school will also reveal any discipline problems and help you learn about academic achievements. This will keep father-son or father-daughter long-distance interactions far more enjoyable and insightful.

• Similarly, an occasional telephone call to their sports coaches and music instructors will display your appreciation for their love and attention to your child.

• Keep your children in touch with relatives and friends on your side of the family as much as possible.

• Guard against letting those hours you used to spend with your children each week become absorbed by other activities. Noting your children's special days or events on a calendar will help you keep in touch. Ask their school and PTA to put you on the parent's mailing list.

• Keep a camera handy and regularly enclose snapshots of yourself at home or at work.

Smart Idea:
Once a week have everyone scour your house for loose change—pockets, dresser tops, couches, car seats (no piggy banks, though). Put the coins in a jar. Once the total reaches fifteen or twenty dollars, vote on an activity for the "Loose Change Party"—miniature golf, buying a new board game or read-aloud book, etc.

Maximize Your Moments of Weakness

Even when you are at your fathering worst, you can enhance your relationship with your child. Your child must know your failures as well as your strengths. It is through your weaknesses that your kids will understand guilt, forgiveness, and rebounding from falling away—however slight or serious your fall was. To let a child see you walk through the consequences of a sorry choice is more powerful than pretending you don't falter morally. Your child needs to observe you facing problems of your own making with courage.

For your kids will need your forgiveness, too. They will seek your forgiveness more readily if they have seen you seek forgiveness for your failings. It is simply not true that if fathers reveal personal weaknesses, their children will lose respect for them. To the contrary: When you are man enough to admit you are wrong, own your mistake, and make the turnaround—then you will garner your children's deep respect.

Maximize the Big Moments in Your Child's Life

We've talked a lot so far about being a presence in your children's day-to-day routine—playtimes, mealtimes, bedtimes. Yet your absence is extra-obvious if you miss the big events—the birthdays, recitals, performances, the big game. Granted, more character is shaped, more life skills are communicated during the seemingly insignificant events in life. Yet children interpret your participation in their big moments as a measure of your love.

How do you know what a "big" moment is for your child? Just look at it from their perspective. How do *they* view the event?

Birthdays may be the most significant celebrations of a child. So invest generous amounts of time—and of yourself—in making special birthday memories. Make it *the* event that tells your child that you're glad beyond words that she is alive.

Plan "Trophy Moments"

These are times of celebrating your child's achievements—and each achievement gives you another chance to heighten his sense of competency. Teetering around the block for the first time on a two-wheeler (training wheels removed), scoring an A on an English test, earning a Boy Scout merit badge, graduation of any sort—these are trophy moments.

Take plenty of snapshots at trophy moments, and keep them in a special photo album—maybe label it "Sharon's Achievements." As she grows up, she can recall the evidence that she is capable and can accomplish the things she sets out to do. This photographic record makes a rare and precious gift for her when she leaves home.

Create your own big moments to reward your kids. I've taken each of my kids to Washington, D.C., with me. We spend two or three or four days together, studying the history of our country. During these trips I have shared my own values more deeply with them and given them my perspective of all we see.

But your big moments don't have to be extravagant—just special for both you and your children.

Maximize the Moments of Crisis

A crisis is opportunity as well as danger. I hope your secretary or receptionist knows that you *always* want a call from your children put through immediately. Do your kids have an extra quarter in a pocket or shoe with your work phone number taped on it? Or do they know your calling-card number? If there's going to be a crisis, be there. Whoever is with your child during a crisis will strongly influence the direction your child's life takes.

Take Time to Beat the Competition

Face it—most of us are competitive. The rap is well-deserved and, probably, one you are proud of. So at least harness it to work on behalf of your kids. A world full of diverse forces are competing hard against you for your kids' minds and hearts. Some of these forces are obvious; they pack a gun or a baseball bat or a pill or a six-pack. But usually the battle isn't nearly as clear as this. And you can't win it by default, either. By maximizing your moments—that is, by spending time with your children—you can monitor the media and peers that compete for your kids' attention. Such forces never let up—and you shouldn't, either.

10

Nicks, Scrapes, and Gouges
Taking Your Habits on the Road

The frenzy had begun just before Wayne arrived home from a three-day business trip. Casper the hamster had somehow escaped from his cage; the kids guessed he was hiding under the couch. The couch was too heavy for Mom to lift, so it had to wait until Dad came home. Wayne had scarcely removed his coat before he got the whole story. So he stepped to the couch and raised one end so his daughter could look for Casper.

There he was, all right. But he darted out of his hiding place and skittered across the living room floor.

No one had noticed Samson trot into the room, attracted by all the commotion. When the black Labrador saw the scurrying hamster, he saw the chance of his canine lifetime. He lunged at Casper and, with a snap of his jaws, killed the poor rodent on the spot.

Horrified, the kids screamed and cried. Wayne yelled at Samson, who was oblivious to everything but his carnivorous instincts and the thrill of fresh blood. In short, the lab dismembered Casper in front of everyone. It took a long while to calm the kids, clean up the mess, and restore a degree of order to the household.

After he comforted his kids, Wayne called a family meeting. The agenda: to determine what had happened and to ensure it wouldn't happen again. Being the latecomer onto the scene, he released a downpour of paternal questioning: "Okay, who left the hamster cage door open? Who played with him last? Who didn't close the back door that the dog came through?"

The kids had some questions of their own: "Why didn't Casper come to me? Why did Samson eat Casper? Why aren't you spanking Samson?" The upshot was, everyone gradually owned up to their responsibilities when the now-docile Samson, sitting off to the side, started gagging. He vomited up the hamster right there at their feet.

There are some moments for which no fathering model can prepare us. There is no textbook way to handle spontaneous domestic traumas, such as Wayne's fiasco with Casper and Samson. Real-life fathering can be messy. Don't think for a minute that the five key habits of smart dads will make your fathering experience neat and tidy. What it will do, though, is assist you to your destination: a mutually satisfying relationship with your kids and, eventually, a positive imprint on their lives.

I don't hang around auto tire stores any more than the next guy. But the other day I took my youngest son with me to have a set of tires mounted on my car. In the waiting area I leafed through a couple brochures and was surprised again by the diversity of rims and tread designs available. Kevin and I ran our fingers along the groove patterns in the rubber. We felt the smooth, shiny contours at the chrome rim display. And Kevin did his usual twenty-questions drill on me: "What's this? What's it for? Why . . . ?"

The tires and rims were showroom fresh compared to the used wheels being worked on in the service bays twenty feet away. Wheels—rims as well as tires—take a pounding from speed bumps and curbs, roads under construction, potholes, the constant stress of starts and stops, intersection drainage dips. Through rainstorms and winter slush, emergency stops and hard cornering, we depend on those lug nuts, rims, tires, and tread to do the job and keep us safe.

After only a few thousand miles, wheels start losing their sheen. But they acquire a different kind of beauty—the look of a well-used tool. Nicked, gouged, and tarnished here and there from the use, but still rock solid.

I see fathering like that. When the five fathering habits are in place, working properly, you can handle whatever family conditions life presents, though you'll inevitably pick up nicks, scrapes, and gouges.

Smart Idea:
Once in a while surprise your family by coming home a day early from a trip. Or cancel a whole day of work (or even just a morning) to be with them. If your wife works, coordinate schedules so that everyone can be together.

Maybe you like what you've read so far about what it takes to be a smart dad. I'll assume that you're sold on the habits. But liking what you see and getting these habits established in yourself are two different things. Let's look at what it will take to get them functioning productively in you.

Balance Those Wheels!

After a tire is mounted and before it's put back on your car, it's usually balanced so that it spins smoothly and doesn't vibrate at high speeds causing excessive stress and wear. Balancing your fathering, accordingly, means examining the strength and balance of the elements in your fathering network to be sure things are in sync.

Try this self-test to check your fathering balance:

Network area	*Current level of strength*
	Poor Excellent
1. I understand the strengths and weaknesses of my fathering personality.	1 2 3 4 5 6 7 8 9 10
2. I have good coping strategies in place to compensate for my natural weaknesses.	1 2 3 4 5 6 7 8 9 10
3. I have a clear understanding of my child's personality strengths and weaknesses and how they tend to play against my own.	1 2 3 4 5 6 7 8 9 10
4. I regularly discuss my child's progress with his mom and value her insight into both the child and my fathering practices.	1 2 3 4 5 6 7 8 9 10
5. I have at least two good friends I talk candidly with at least once a month.	1 2 3 4 5 6 7 8 9 10
6. I have made meaningful contact within the last two months with adults who relate regularly to my child (teachers, coaches, bosses, neighbors, scout leaders, etc.)	1 2 3 4 5 6 7 8 9 10
7. I have read a book, listened to a tape, or attended a seminar about fathering in the past twelve months.	1 2 3 4 5 6 7 8 9 10

Alignment

Unaligned front wheels cause stress, excessive wear, and instability to the entire steering system. Likewise, you need to align fathering with your other roles—husband, employee or owner, son of elderly parents, weekend tennis player, bass fishing enthusiast, soccer coach—that you fulfill in your family, company, and community. Keeping these various responsibilities and pressure points in alignment is what challenges and frustrates most fathers.

You will succeed as a dad only if you take the time to carefully consider how much time, energy, and money you are willing to commit to each of these roles in your life.

You may be like me. Every time I sit down and review where I am in my fathering growth and practices, I uncover more adjustments—more alignments—that I need to make. And I've learned that I can either practice good maintenance and do the alignment *right then*, or I can put it off and try not to think about what I know without a doubt—that someday it will take a lot more time and expense to get the alignment put back where it should have been all along.

Say you realize that things aren't clicking like they should between you and your child. You're not getting the attention and response you expect when you advise or instruct her. Your instincts (or a discussion with her mother) tell you what the underlying problem is: Your schedule over the past couple months hasn't left you with much time with her. Communication levels are consequently down. All the child has been hearing from you are commands and demands. So it's no wonder that her responsiveness toward you in general has shriveled.

What your fathering needs right then is realignment with your other roles. You probably need to spend more time with your child. So being the wise father that you are, you make the tough decision to cut back on the extra hours you are putting in at the office or on a community service project or on the golf course or whatever.

I know what I'm talking about. Three times in the past week I was annoyed with responses I've gotten from one or the other of my sons when I asked them to follow through on a chore. My knee-jerk reaction was "What's wrong with this kid?" A calmer look at their resistance to my fathering revealed that, for the past four months, I've devoted a *lot* of extra time to writing this book. Special times with the boys have been too scarce. Their lackluster response to my commands turned out to be no mystery at all. So now I'm making the adjustments to bring my fathering back into alignment.

Realignment is managing critical and competing responsibilities. That's probably why it's difficult. For instance, you see your overtime hours on the job as discretionary—not a part of your job description. So you figure after all these extra hours at the office for months on end, it's your kids' turn to get some extra attention from you.

Yet just because you adjusted your fathering priority doesn't mean your boss has to agree with you. He may or may not perceive your overtime and extra efforts as discretionary. Your most recent raise, in fact, may have been awarded you with the unspoken expectation of more sixty- and seventy-hour weeks.

Realignment of fathering and career will take some tactful discussion in a situation like this. You may or may not want to explain that you are changing how you work in order to accommodate your new fathering focus. I'd suggest being forthright; you never know the positive effect it may have.

A friend who worked for a savings and loan was assigned a loan analysis by his boss at about four in the afternoon, with the request to have it ready for a board meeting the next morning. Normally he would have stayed late and completed the work. But he had been working hard during the past month to bring his fathering priorities into better alignment. And working that evening conflicted with his son's soccer game, which he had promised to attend.

So my friend swallowed hard and explained it all to his boss: Normally he'd be happy to stay late, but this particular evening he had made a promise to his son that he didn't want to break.

The boss was accommodating—but the real reaction came the next day. The boss told my friend that seeing him make fathering a priority had made him think hard about the way work had become too important in his own life. So, he said, he was instituting a policy that no one stayed beyond six, except for Thursdays. And he was having the building's security system adjusted accordingly, so that if you left after six the alarms would create all kinds of havoc.

You'll always be realigning, because the patterns and habits of our lives always take time, energy, and money. When you adjust or change a habit in one dimension, something will have to give somewhere else.

Good Tire Maintenance

Because your four tires each wear a little differently, you rotate them regularly to get the most wear from them. In the same way, as you cycle through different

Smart Idea:
Ask another dad to tell you the fathering mistakes he wants to avoid and the fathering examples he hopes to emulate.

seasons of life—new fatherhood, career change, your kids' adolescence, a new marriage—fathering will be at the front of your attention sometimes, and be on the back burner at others.

Once you establish the five key habits of a smart dad, practicing them will become much easier. What you do out of habit isn't difficult. Good fathering habits will keep you moving and in control even during those seasons when your attention is required elsewhere.

No Modifications Necessary

I've met fathers who, from what I've observed of their behavior, think of fathering as a competitive sport. They want to be the biggest and the best. So they adopt an attitude akin to putting slicks on a race car. Looks hot, but the down side of this modification is that fathering is not a drag race. Slicks just don't do well in a race of endurance. Whatever habits we acquire should keep working powerfully for a lifetime. So here's my advice:

• **Don't pretend to be more or better than you are as a man or a father.** If you fool everyone else, at least your children will know the truth—and of all people, they're the ones who need to see a transparent, frank father.

• **Don't compete with other fathers.** Nothing spoils a healthy relationship with your network faster. Keep other fathers as your allies, not as contestants.

• **Presenting yourself as a larger-than-life dad wears down you and those around you.** Do you do things more in the interest of your fathering reputation than in the best interest of your children? A friend of mine—father of four and the associate pastor of a church—asks himself that question often. Some in his congregation expect him to be an exemplary father—and he knows how easily he can oblige them, at least in appearances. He says he used to worry more that he *looked* like a good dad than actually *being* a good dad.

It's Never Too Soon to Start Good Fathering Habits

Women get a head start in parenting. The changes in their bodies demand that they start adapting to the baby months before it arrives. Dads, on the other hand, experience no biological changes that demand we start adjusting to the responsibility. It takes a conscious effort for us to prepare for the expectations and requirements of fatherhood.

It's never too early to start the thought patterns and habits that make you a smart dad. In fact, here are some ideas for bonding with your unborn child (if you have the opportunity):

• **Write a letter to your unborn child.** Express the joy and anticipation you feel as a parent. Write of your desire to parent the baby. Verbalize the desires that have led you and your wife to want to have a child. Put into words your hope for the kind of person you trust the child will become.

Then put the letter in a safe deposit box to be opened on the child's twelfth birthday. Your long-term goal is to build your child's sense of self-worth with the assurance that his or her arrival was a welcomed event.

• **Sing and talk to your unborn child.** Unborn babies hear sounds and respond to them. Let that little one get to know the sound of your voice before it sees your face.

• **Feel your baby move.** Take time to lay your hands on your wife's abdomen and wait until your little one makes a move.

• **Accompany your wife on her prenatal visits.** Watching an ultrasound image or listening to the heartbeat of your unborn child heightens the reality of that growing life.

Once your baby is born, take an active role in child-rearing. The new version of Dr. Benjamin Spock's *Baby and Child Care* offers this advice: "The father—any father—should be sharing with the mother the day-to-day care of their child from birth onward. . . . This is the natural way for the father to start the relationship, just as it is for the mother."[1]

Your decision to participate in your child's early development will pay rich dividends. Research regularly shows that when a child's father involves himself early in child rearing, children tend to have higher IQs, perform better in school, and even have a better sense of humor than children whose fathers do not give themselves and their children this advantage.[2]

Specifically, you can bond with your newborn in ways like this:

• **Let the baby learn your comforting techniques.** Snuggle your baby's head up under your chin, then talk and sing to it

Smart Idea:
If you're unsure of the answers to these and similar questions, go ahead and ask your child.
• What most embarrasses your child?
• Who (outside your home) most influences him or her?
• What is your child's biggest fear?
• What is your child's most prized possession?
If you need to get the conversation going, first tell them what embarrasses, influences, and frightens you.

in low masculine tones. Your infant will learn to be comforted by your style just as he or she responds to Mom's touch.

• **Read some child-development literature—or at least some articles in baby magazines.** (Baby mags and mailers will flood your home when infant-product companies learn you've just had a baby.) Become familiar with your baby's coming developmental signs. (In fact, try beating Mom at noticing a new stage in the baby.)

• **Take your shirt off when you hold the baby.** Skin is your newborn's primary sensory channel. Feeling the warmth of your chest, just as when Mom nurses the child, greatly enhances the bonding and the ability to feel comforted by you.

Two Ways to Get New Habits Rolling

Focus on improvement rather than perfection.

Consider each of the five habits as a continuum, as a range. Pinpoint as closely as you can where you currently are in practicing the five key habits of smart dads—then aim for measurable improvement, not perfection. If you aim too high too soon, you will probably procrastinate rather than attempt progress.

List your ideas for putting each of these five key habits into action.

Nothing disciplines one's thinking like the point of a pencil. Written commitments afford you the valuable opportunity of confronting yourself later in your own handwriting about what you did or did not do.

You may want to start like this: Divide a sheet of paper into three columns. In the left column list the five key habits. In the center write your expressed goal regarding that habit. In the right column list specific steps you will take to reach that goal. (See page 158 for an example.)

The goals and action steps, of course, will shift in tone and focus the older your child becomes. Brainstorm for action steps with a friend or your wife, listing as many specific steps as you can. Then be very selective, however, and try only a few changes at one time. Biting off more than

Smart Idea:
Reduce petty arguments and sibling rivalry with a "Child of the Week" strategy. The privileged child gets to choose the prime seat in the car, operate the garage door opener, push the shopping cart, and spend Saturday afternoon alone with dad and his favorite game or activity.

you can chew only sets you up for failure. It is not how many changes you institute that matters, but the number of habits you develop that become a part of your everyday routine. Start small and exceed your expectations. Regularly building on your last accomplishments as a dad can take you, over the course of a lifetime, to fathering heights you didn't imagine were possible.

This will take you less than a minute, so do it now, before you turn the page or lay this book down: Consider your fathering goals and options. Choose one, simple, workable action step—one that you have listed above, or another than comes to mind. Now get up and do it, right now, before the idea becomes cold.

FIVE KEY HABITS OF SMART DADS

Key Habit	Goal	Action Steps
1. Grasp my significance	Create in my children the positive memory of my being there for them as they grow up.	Remind myself three times today that just being there for my kids and being affectionate makes a world of difference.
2. Act intentionally	Revise my schedule to accommodate new fathering focus and goals.	Set aside two hours, sometime in the next week, to plan how I will apply what I have learned in this book.
3. Use my network	Build primary and secondary fathering networks.	Discuss these five key habits with my wife and ask her to evaluate my strengths and weaknesses. Then find two other fathers with whom I can meet regularly as a support group.
4. Communicate life skills and principles	Have my children know what skills and principles they each are working on, and be proud of their individual achievements.	List the things I want to teach my kids before they leave home. Find and use three teachable moments in the life of each child this week.
5. Maximize my moments	Learn to consistently harness small moments of time in fathering.	Add one item to my daily routine with each child. Play with my kids fifteen minutes each day.

NICKS, SCRAPES, AND GOUGES

Key Habit	Goal	Action Steps
1. Grasp my significance		
2. Act intentionally		
3. Use my network		
4. Communicate life skills and principles		
5. Maximize my moments		

11

Burnin' Rubber

The Tire Track: Your Fathering Legacy

I got hit in a fender bender last Saturday. No one was hurt, but the other car creased my rear quarter panel behind the wheel well. The driver, who had turned out of a shopping-center driveway onto the road without noticing me, was embarrassed and frustrated at having caused her first accident. Skid marks five or six feet long, made by my tires when I was hit, attested to the force she bumped me with.

The skid of an accident or of a panic stop, the cautious progress of a four-wheel drive through mud, raising dust as you bump along on a dirt road—in the right circumstances, tires leave a clear signature. In the same way, your fathering legacy is the record of those moments and experiences you share with your child. An imprint.

I'm famous in my house for recognizing what good fathering means to my kids, framing a plan, putting it in writing—and then gliding along on the strength of my good intentions. Meanwhile, a dangerous gap grows between my great plan and my actual performance. In fathering, as in most aspects of life, it's performance that counts, not wonderful intentions. Tire tracks aren't left behind where the tire never rolled.

It's one thing to admire a showroom tire, glistening black, hard edges on all the tread, mounted on the latest style rim. It's another

Five Key Habits of Smart Dads
FATHERING PARADIGM

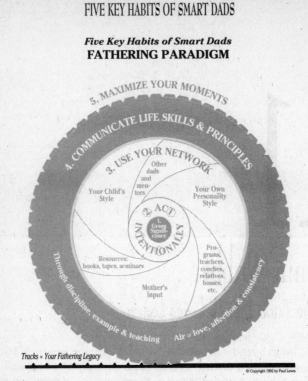

5. MAXIMIZE YOUR MOMENTS

4. COMMUNICATE LIFE SKILLS & PRINCIPLES

3. USE YOUR NETWORK

Other dads and mentors

Your Child's Style

Your Own Personality Style

2. ACT INTENTIONALLY

1. Grasp Significance

Pro-grams, teachers, coaches, relatives, bosses, etc.

Resources: books, tapes, seminars

Mother's Input

Through discipline, example & teaching

Air = love, affection & consistency

Tracks = Your Fathering Legacy

© Copyright 1992 by Paul Lewis

thing, though, to put that tire on a pickup and send it off to thirty or forty thousand miles of daily wear and tear. Then you find out how good it is. Fathering habits, too, look nice when you showcase them. But they'll work for you only if you put them on, use them every day on life's road, keep them in good repair and road-ready month after month, year after year.

Preventive Fathering

Often it's just forgetting commonsense prevention that gets dads into fathering trouble. If you don't practice preventive father-ing, you'll end up playing catch-up or trying to compensate for an outright mistake you made earlier.

"It's a whole lot cheaper to prevent disease than it is to treat them," says Dr. Kenneth Cooper, who popularized aerobic exercise. "It's a whole lot cheaper to prevent family problems than it is to heal them. Whether it's drug addiction, alcohol, obesity, heart dis-ease—we as parents should be keenly concerned in the potential of preventive medicine for our families."

Likewise, preventive fathering can protect you from problems that damage father-child relationships.

You've seen the scenario—a scrubbed, cheerful, clean-cut mechanic (or plumber, contractor, etc.) in a pressed uniform hands a customer the bill. "That will be $49.95 for the check-up," he says politely. The appreciative customer drives off, thoroughly satisfied. Cut to a greasy mechanic—filthy jumpsuit, matted hair, a day or two of stubble on his face—who, with a smirk, hands a cowering customer the oily bill. The customer's face registers shock, and you know why. Cut to Mr. Clean again, who warns us that "in maintaining your car, you have a choice: you can pay *me* now . . . or you can pay *him* later."

You can invest in your children up front—it's fairly manageable to attend to each of their stages as they come along—or you can neglect your relationship with your kids when they're young and later pay far more than you can afford.

Preventive fathering means monitoring these habits:

Check the pressure level in your various roles monthly.

You can't avoid pressures in this life—but is your life overinflated? Avoid a blowout—release some of your commitments, even if you have to drop *good* things. Overcommitment, contends Focus on the Family founder James Dobson, is the single most damaging habit of families today. Police yourself so you don't overload your life with too many commitments and activities.

Drive at moderate speeds, observing legal limits.

Safer, more satisfying fathering comes easier as you move slowly. Don't hurry your children to grow up too soon. Let each grow at his or her appropriate pace. Don't rush yourself, either. Take time to develop the skills, knowledge, and habits that allow you to father your children well.

Mistakes happen when we hurry. Discern and accept the natural limitations on you and on each of your children, and you can relax and enjoy the ride *during* their childhood.

Smart Tip:

These rules can lead to fair solutions in resolving problems between family members:

1. Anyone can call a family-council meeting.

2. Everyone is free to say what he or she thinks about a situation.

3. Blaming is not allowed in determining why a problem exists.

4. The solution must be fair to all.

Avoid driving over potholes, obstacles, curbs, or edges of pavement.

Awareness in fathering is like good defensive driving: You anticipate obstacles before they hit you.

Are you now anticipating the issues your child will face in his next stage of life? What type of questions will she begin asking? Are you prepared? Do you have a clue how you will answer her? What will he need most from you? Do you know any of the early warning signs for errant behavior (like substance abuse or depression)? Are you an alert father?

Notice obstacles up ahead, and you will be in the envious position to deal with them before they hit you.

Avoid spinning your wheels.

That is, don't make a lot of promises to your wife and kids that you don't back up with action. Big plans and no delivery is just like burning rubber: You generate a lot of fury and noise, but it doesn't get you anywhere.

Don't spout off about what you plan to do. It doesn't matter if it's swearing off alcohol, a Disneyland vacation, or threats of dire punishment to an erring child. If you have no sure plan of making good your promise or threat, keep quiet. Steady, measured, intentional actions, without fanfare, are usually the better course.

"If you see any damage to a tire," reads the brochure of a tire manufacturer, "replace it with a spare and see a tire-care professional at once."[1]

Few families escape without some kind of serious damage to relationships—medical emergencies, clinical depression, emotional difficulties, addiction, abuse of whatever kind, victimization within the family or from outside.

When it feels like a blowout, don't ignore it and barrel ahead. Pull over and get competent professional help.

Prepare for All Driving Conditions

Be prepared to make necessary adjustments for various driving conditions:

Off-road driving

There will be times in your life when you take an unexpected turn with a child and realize you've turned off the road altogether.

BURNIN' RUBBER

You thought your map had everything marked, but you can't find where you are now. You're off-roading as a father.

I think of the U.S. Army general who testified before the Senate Armed Services Committee, offering his recommendation against allowing homosexuals to serve in the military. The night before, this dad's adult son called him to tell him he was gay.

That was an off-road moment for the father. He had probably never prepared himself for such a situation. Yet the next day before the Senate committee, he responded with love and respect for his son while remaining true to his convictions.

I started some of my own off-roading the day I found proof that my oldest son was smoking marijuana. I never believed I would have to deal with this; the fathering maps I had studied (and taught) didn't chart that territory. I had mistakenly thought that fathers who made good choices were guaranteed sons who did, too.

We were living in a small mountain community—oaks, pines, meadow ponds, country roads—an ideal environment in which to raise children, I thought.

Yet from day one, Jon had been a risk taker. He climbed pine trees higher than you would imagine a six- or eight-year-old could climb. He loved the adventure, the risk of it.

Jon was bright—really—but by junior high, a learning disability diagnosed in third grade was taking a toll. Although he could ace a verbal test, he had great difficulty encoding what he knew in written form—the common measure of classroom progress. His coping mechanisms were no longer handling the volume of written work required.

Few of Jon's friends in this small community shared the values of our family. Combine Jon's love of experimenting, his learning difficulty, the trauma of even a *smooth* adolescence—and you've got the perfect recipe for a problem. Jon succumbed, and it took us a while to figure it all out.

I relied heavily during those two years on my fathering network. I got a lot of good counsel from other fathers who had already navigated this territory. (More about Jon's story in chapter twelve.)

Even if a father does *everything* right (and I didn't), there is no guarantee that

Smart Idea:
Strengthen family ties on birthdays and anniversaries by playing "Family Trivia." Stump the kids with questions like these:
- In what year were we married?
- How old is grandpa?
- Name your great-grandparents.
- Who is your oldest cousin?

all his children will turn out just as he thinks they should be. Such a guarantee is a fantasy that will lull you into a state of denial. You simply cannot control every factor that comes along to challenge your fathering. Reality, on the other hand, teaches me that, while there are no guarantees, I can tilt the odds in my favor by living out these five fathering habits.

Driving when drowsy—nodding off or not paying attention

There's a lot of semiconscious fathering going on, despite the fact that it's a dangerous way to live with a family. If you're not paying attention or are simply too tired (in any sense of the word) to father well, pull over, and get some rest—before you run off the road.

Avoiding road hazards

When I was growing up in Dayton, Ohio, I remember city street crews waging their annual battle against the potholes created by the winter freezing and thawing. A family friend was among the first buyers of a VW beetle, and we'd joke about him getting lost in a pothole.

There are serious road hazards out there. For some fathers, it's emotional (or worse) abuse of wives and children, or workaholism. For your children, it's gang involvement, recreational drug use, alcohol abuse, promiscuous sex, AIDS, abortion, molestation.

Blessed are the children with alert fathers who help them steer clear of hazards that can maim the body and the spirit.

When road signs point in the wrong direction

Road Runner, you remember, would flip the road sign so that Wile E. Coyote, mistakenly following the arrow, careened off the cliff.

Among modern road signs that misdirect our kids:

• **Evolution.** When we tell children that life began as blind chance, that their significance lies in being simply the latest play in a huge survival-of-the-fittest game, we shouldn't be surprised when they abuse each other or join racist groups that vaunt their own superiority. If evolution is your philosophical core, there is little reason for shaping a sense of positive worth and self-esteem, or for valuing the person next to you. We must teach children that each of them are special because they have been created by God and endowed with a unique purpose for their lives.

From this premise—the purposeful creation of all life by God—springs all other values that make life sacred.

• **Safe sex.** We put kids at great risk by teaching them that condoms eliminate the risk of AIDS and of sexually transmitted diseases. Condoms fail at an astounding rate. If, as a hundred passengers prepared to board a plane in Los Angeles for Chicago, the attendant announced that about eighty-three would make it safely and the rest would die, how many passengers would go aboard?

Only abstinence is absolutely safe. The safe-sex sell is a tragic hoax. For a score of other reasons besides catching a deadly disease, what loving father wouldn't strongly warn his children that choosing to be sexually active before marriage is a monstrous risk?

Modern society has flipped lots more warning signs, so that now our children are told that whatever is legal is moral, that pornography is a harmless adult pleasure, that gender roles are interchangeable. Your job as a dad is to hear where society wants to escort your children, clearly interpret it, and carefully and tactfully lead children to see through the illogical, fuzzy thinking.

Fathering Myths and Mistakes

I've been a father now for a quarter century. More important, I've listened to the perspective of thousands of fathers. From their combined experience, I have identified several myths and mistakes that are poised to defeat us. When repeated consistently—or even when left unexamined—these four myths and four mistakes can run you off the fathering road.

Myth 1: Big Moments Count Most

When I feel like I'm behind in my relationship with my children, I tend to look for some grand moment I can create to catch up, to fix the problem—to at least absolve my sense of guilt about not being there enough. It's the whole evening we'll spend together (later in the week), the big Saturday outing (in two weeks), the extravagant vacation together that will make a lifetime memory (next summer)—anything to make up for the time I'm not investing in the relationship right now.

Smart Tip:
Manage TV viewing time. Balance it with reading, chores, music practice, homework, whatever. Track a child's TV time with a jar of marbles on top of the tube: A marble is deposited in the jar for each half hour of reading, chores, etc. A glance at the jar lets people know how much TV watching the child has earned.

Big moments are important, but not as much as you think. It's fantasy to believe that they count most in shaping a relationship with kids. The truth is that lots of small moments count for more. Children's values, memories, and habits are shaped one moment and one day at a time. When a question is on your son's mind, he'll ask it—then. They're around twelve before they can put an emotional need on hold for a few days until you are around to respond to it. Small children can't wait for even a day. They need you when they need you. To wait for tomorrow night is an eternity to them.

If we're not around to answer their life questions, others will be. That's reality.

Myth 2: Strong Fathers Stand Alone

American lore says that a real man always knows what to do in every situation. He handles crises without consulting anyone or anything. Dads like to pack this myth home—so we work in isolation, seldom asking each other about what makes for strong fathering and healthy marriages.

We take the one shot we get at raising each of our kids—a highwire act without a net of other strong fathers and mentors who can coach us. For whatever reasons, we honor independence, not interdependence.

The truth is, every man needs connections to others. A network of healthy relationships enriches his ability to father. I am a better father because of the hours I've spent across a table with other dads (a point I made in chapter seven about using your network).

Myth 3: Pain Is Pointless

Love for our children makes it almost understandable to want to shield them from every pain. Yet in so doing, we also shield them from powerful lessons learned only through making their own mistakes and slugging it out through consequent difficulties. Saturated in our culture with the message that sacrifice and suffering are needless, we are not encouraged to lower the shield. Yet if we believe that pain is pointless, we lose a great source of wisdom. Mistakes are powerful tutors.

Every family and individual will experience pain, in some form or another—physical, emotional, mental. Pain is regularly the natural consequence of a poor choice or mistake. And, of course, some pain just happens.

If we respond positively to suffering, it has a beautiful and refining effect on our character. While never engineering a trauma for his child, a wise father nevertheless knows that his child's suffering is a painful, valuable opportunity to learn life skills and values. So with a careful eye to what is enough and what is too much, he usually allows the logical and natural consequences of his child's mistakes to fall on him or her.

The child who learns that lemonade can be made from life's lemons—that there is a point to life's pains—has a huge advantage over individuals who seek to avoid every difficulty.

Myth 4: Great Fathering Is Just Around the Corner

This myth seduces young fathers in particular, although at careless moments I still give in to it.

Here's how it often works. We deliberately choose imbalance ("just for a while") to make the career move, win the promotion, close the big deal, get the new business up and running. Time with our children? Well, you'll get right on it—as soon as you finish this *really* important project.

The truth is that as soon as you get around this corner, you're probably looking at another corner, no less critical to get around than the last one.

Today's economic climate makes things less certain than ever. Companies downsize, folding two or three jobs into yours—and twenty people lined up for your job are perfectly willing to put in the overtime if you aren't. If you hustle less in order to be available to your children, somebody else will win the contract or close the deal.

Life is compromise—and there will be seasons of compromising fathering time. But at least you can keep your thinking clear and recognize the downside of any decisions to temporarily postpone time with your kids.

If we're lucky, we get about twenty years of fathering a child. Just one shot. I've talked to too many fathers who regret moments they wish they could have shared with their children. Your kids are two years old just once. They're five, then nine, then fourteen just once. Questions burn in their heads, begging for answers—at just this moment, just that day. Only once do they hit their first home run, turn sixteen, or endure their first romantic breakup. A wise father learns to value each

Smart Idea:
Ask "seesaw" questions at dinner tonight:
• Did you feel today more like a heart or a brain? A washer or dryer? A steak or a hamburger?
• Do you think our family is more like a factory or a farm? A TV or a newspaper? The city or the country?
• Why?

day as if it was the only one he will have with his children. He avoids pretending that he'll have more time later, when he'll be freed up to be a great dad. He values most the moments he has now with his kids.

When I ask older dads what their greatest regret is—and I ask this often—I've never heard, "I regret I didn't pursue my career more intensely." But lots of men say, in one way or another, "I regret that I didn't take more time for my kids when they were young and available to me and craved the interaction. What I traded for those moments wasn't worth it."

Four Common Fathering Mistakes

Mistake 1: Demanding Common Ground on Your Turf

Don't push your children into activities that are more *your* interest than your child's. We all know the caricature of the dad who lives out his athletic fantasies in his child. None of us wants that.

Yet kids so love their dads' involvement and approval that they will push themselves to excel at what they guess (usually accurately) will earn them Dad's admiration—even if it's not what they genuinely enjoy or want to do.

That's as unhealthy as the overtly pushy father. Instead, look at your children's abilities and interests, then find some authentically common ground—an interest, a pastime, a recreation that both father and child sincerely enjoy. Athletics may not be the best common turf. Maybe it will be piano or photography or electronics or modeling or collecting. It may be something you find boring; for when there seem to be no areas of overlapping interest, a dad needs to be sufficiently wise to choose the child's turf over his own.

Since he was two, my youngest son's passion has been mechanical things—in particular, cranes, earth movers, even the fork lifts at the wholesale building-supply warehouse we shop in. So I made Kevin the perfect invitation: to come with me to the Caterpillar dealership's used-equipment lot. Acres of earth-moving equipment, waiting to be mauled and scrambled on by a young boy enthralled with machinery.

Sure, the equipment interested me—for a few minutes. Hydraulic fluid and grease aren't my idea of a great Saturday morning. But Kevin's delight poking around those machines with me tells me we're on common ground—which is where an effective father needs to spend some time.

Mistake 2: Expecting Adult Behavior and Reasoning Too Early

A dad usually expects more mature behavior than his kids are able to deliver. So he gets all exasperated about something they should have done and didn't, or at least didn't do to his expectations. *They* knew exactly what he wanted done, and yet they didn't do it. So he raises his voice and launches into an adult's classic string of interrogatives: "How many times have I told you . . . ?" "How come you never . . . ?" "Why can't you ever . . . ?" "Why don't you act your age?" and "Surely you realize . . ."

These are nothing less than put-downs, and they seldom spur children toward mature behavior. The most they usually accomplish—besides making us feel better about getting it off our chest—is to make our child feel as capable as a whipped puppy.

The problem is usually mine, not my child's. When I tell my daughter, "Your room is a disaster—clean it this afternoon," I set up Shelley for failure. Unless she and I have established beyond doubt what constitutes a clean room, her idea of a clean room and my idea of a clean room can be far apart. So she produces an award-winning clean room, by her definition. Then I show up to inspect, only to end up yelling, "Shelley, get in here! I thought I told you to clean up your room!"

That's when I let emotion overwhelm logic. That's when I belittle my child.

All I needed to do to avoid the misunderstanding was to clarify my expectations up front. When I first assigned the clean-up task, I should have asked Shelley to stand with me in the doorway of her room for a moment and describe the way the room will look when clean. I should have let her talk me through the job as she sees it. If she missed something, I could have simply asked, "And what about those clothes hanging out of the drawer—is the room 'clean' if they're still there?"

Questions like these clarify a task for your child and help her succeed in living up to your expectations.

Once you have taught her how to perform the task, it is fair to expect her to do it as you have taught her. If she doesn't, you have a legitimate gripe. Then you

Smart Idea:
When you know you'll arrive home after your child's bedtime, ask her to jot on a Post-It any questions, requests, or comments for you—and stick it on the bathroom mirror. And if you leave in the morning before they awake, leave your response on their mirror.

calmly ask her what standards she agreed to, and ask her to finish the job.

Mistake 3: A Short Fuse and Explosive Anger

When I talk shop with experienced dads, I ask them what they are least proud of in their fathering. By far, the most common answers are uncontrolled anger and a quick temper. "I can have a very short fuse," they'll say, "and I'm not proud of it." Repeated outbursts of anger usually reflect an internal problem—his own impatience or suppressed rage. Though he blows up at his child, the child was hardly the fundamental cause of his anger.

Adult anger is seldom a productive emotion in the presence of children. Uncontrolled anger at a child tears at her respect for her father and erects instant barriers against him. You don't go out of your way to confide in a person who has vented his anger on you a number of times already.

If you have a short fuse, get help—and start with your spouse. Some couples have a subtle signal they use to help him keep a lid on his anger. Some agree that, when she senses him losing control, she will get his attention by slamming a door somewhere in the house, or by humming "Dixie"—*anything* that can remind you that you're skating on thin ice.

A couple years in Vietnam left a dad I know with a hair-trigger temper. He feared what damage his tirades might do to his relationships with his three daughters. So after discussing what their dad was grappling with, they made a pact together: Whenever he blew his stack, they would simply grab his hand and, without saying anything, hang on. It was amazing, he told me, how over a few months that one simple act helped calm him.

Whatever approach you adopt, include with it the healthy habit of asking for forgiveness. No matter how justified your anger toward your child may be, logic won't dispel her *feeling* of rejection. Contrary to instinct, a father never stands so tall in his child's eyes as when he admits he's blown it and seeks forgiveness.

Keep short accounts with your family. Don't let years of angry outbursts build walls between you and your children.

Mistake 4: Failure to Choose Your Battles Wisely

If you fight over every little thing with your child, you will eventually lose him. Choose your battles wisely, for it's the important battles you want to win.

Too many dads I talk with are unhappy with the tension between them and their son or daughter—and the cause is merely style. A distinct style (you may call it a horrible style, a decadent style, a silly style) is a normal part of growing children's efforts to express their unique identities. Her current tastes in clothes, music, hair, and room decor may offend you; but these external issues are far less important in the long run than character and integrity. An absence of either can damage your child.

Regardless of how you cringe at being known as the father of a child who dresses or wears her hair as she does, it's better to swallow your pride and save your energy for battles about issues that matter—integrity, loyalty, honesty, keeping your word, choice of friends, education, unsafe or immoral sexual behavior, using drugs, and so forth. Your goal is not compliant, but committed behavior—actions that flow out of the child's personal convictions. You'll gain a lot more of your child's respect when you defend unflinchingly only those things that truly matter.

You don't know what lies ahead on your fathering road. Yet if you instill critical life skills and principles in an atmosphere of love, affection, and consistency through many thousands of encounters and investments of time in the relationship, you will leave behind a clear and strong fathering legacy. The imprint of your life will be clear; your grip into the next generation will be strong and positive. Listen to your network; let them support and encourage you never to give up, especially when the road is rough and your confidence plummets. Every father has those moments. Talk about the journey with others on the fathering road. Lots of fathers have been down the stretch of road you face next.

With the five key habits of smart dads well in place, you are on your way to arriving at your fathering destination safe and secure. But before we part company, there is one other issue I must discuss with you. Your views on this subject affect not only your approach to each of the five fathering habits, but also the level of ultimate success you will experience as a dad. At issue is your foundational view of life and your spiritual moorings.

For me it has been a very personal encounter with God—the heavenly Father—that has enormously impacted in a positive way the quality of my work in each of the five habits. I believe that wise choices in the area of this "supra-factor" produce outstanding results and are key in energizing all the rest.

Let's take a look at how it works . . .

Smart Idea:
Discern where it is that you and your wife or children most easily talk—your bed, their bed, the couch, the car, the back yard, wherever—and return to that setting often.

12

Authentic Father Power
Tapping the Supra-factor

Whew! It was 1:30 A.M., and we were relieved to see our daughter Shona walk in the door. But the tremble in her voice signaled trouble. She had been on a date with her boyfriend—traveling some fifty miles away to San Diego. No call had come to tell us they were going to be late.

More was fueling our anxiety than the lateness of the hour. Shona and Mike had been dating several months. Shona loved Mike's sense of humor, and he was good looking and popular at school. But to us, his troubled background left much to be desired, and it was hard to tell whether he had left all of that as completely as he had assured Shona he had. Even though Mike treated her like a queen, we still weren't thrilled that Shona seemed blind to the dangers we saw in the relationship. I had tried in several conversations to press our views, but to no avail. Although I could lay down the law, I couldn't change Shona's heart about this guy.

Over some hot chocolate the story of the evening tumbled out. It had been a fun date—until the highway patrol pulled them over on their way home. The officer told them cordially that they were driving too slow. As a matter of routine he ran a check on Mike's license number.

When the office returned to the car, his demeanor had changed radically. "Move away from him," he instructed Shona. Then he turned to Mike. "Place your hands on the dashboard," he said. "Do you have any dangerous weapons in your possession?"

He was acting on an outstanding warrant for Mike's arrest, and Shona was pretty sure it wasn't just an unresolved traffic citation. She watched her boyfriend handcuffed and taken into custody on the spot.

The officer asked her if she could get herself home. "Yes," she replied. Shaken to the core, she drove the last twenty-five miles home on an unfamiliar winding mountain road.

Tears were streaming down her face by the time she finished her story. Amid hugs and reassurances, we acknowledged the reality of the situation. Shona had thought that Mike was a neat guy who loved her and had put his past behind him. But our perception as two caring parents that this boyfriend wasn't a good choice had proved to be correct.

Perception vs. Reality

In fathering, just as in every area of life, our perceptions daily dictate what we do and how we respond to each moment and situation. I hear a child's scream from the backyard. My *perception* of its tone and intensity cues me about whether to smile at the good time the kids are having or to run to see who's hurt. When my daughter Shelley says, "You're wrong, Dad," it's my perception of her attitude that either makes me proud of the young woman she is becoming, or makes me worry about a sullen attitude.

Your perceptions about fathering are acted out daily in the judgment calls you make. Can you afford to work late tonight and miss dinner with your family? This one time won't hurt, you figure. It will allow you to give the whole weekend to the kids.

That's a judgment call based on your perception of realities at your house. Fathers make hundreds of these decisions every month, and each one is based on fundamental perceptions about life and how it works.

Your Worldview and Fathering

The collection of ideas, axioms, principles, and beliefs that daily guide your thoughts, decisions, and actions is your worldview. It is how you believe life works. You use this frame of reference to make choices. Even without conscious evaluation, every choice flows from an operating premise you believe will work out best.

Your worldview is also the supra-factor that shapes and impacts your fathering—that overarching element that transcends all other components of your fathering. Your worldview, your belief system affects the quality of your fathering. It's like buttoning a shirt. If you get the top button right, the rest fall in line. If you button that top button in the wrong hole, however, the shirt will be out of alignment.

All this to say that you want your fundamental beliefs, your worldview, your supra-factor, to be as firmly rooted in truth and reality as possible.

I think it is only fair—even important—that I reveal to you my belief system. It seems to me to be the most realistic explanation of the world I experience as a man and father. This worldview honors my role as a father, promotes respect for my wife and children, and guides my understanding of how to act in their best interests. It provides the motivation and power to do what is right when I frankly don't want to do the right thing.

I found this worldview, which in my perspective is firmly rooted in truth and reality, in the Bible. This book explains the selfishness I work so hard to root out of my children, my selfcenteredness that tears at my marriage and fathering. The Bible also explains how to escape from such vices.

I've looked at the historical facts surrounding the birth, life, death, and resurrection of Jesus Christ long and hard. I have carefully weighed the evidence, for I have no intention of being duped or fooled about this. In the process I've been forced to the conclusion that it would require greater faith to disbelieve the Bible than to accept it. The case is simply that strong to me. My decision is to accept it and to encourage my children to do the same.

Your belief system, like mine, colors how you approach each of the five key habits of a smart dad. Let me explain.

The Five Key Habits' Supra-Factor

Among the several definitions of *father* is "Father God"—in my understanding, the true and living God described in the

Smart Idea:
Play "Hug Tag" with your children and the neighborhood kids. Follow regular tag rules, except that players are safe only when they are hugging another player. Then play it again, this time requiring that huggers must be in a *threesome* to be safe; and so on. It's magic!

Old and New Testaments of the Bible, the one who created us, our wives, our children, and who alone is capable of giving family and fatherhood complete and deeply fulfilling meaning. I have found that God is the source of authentic father power.

In fact, God is the ultimate father—his love for his children is unsurpassed, he opens his arms to wayward children who come home, he disciplines his children for their own good.

A little abstract, you say. Agreed—which is why God sent his son, Jesus, into humanity. "Anyone who has seen me has seen the Father," Jesus told his followers (John 14:9), driving the point home even plainer with this declaration: "I and the Father are one" (John 10:30).

Based on a *Psychology Today* survey a few years ago, the magazine's readers named Jesus Christ as the "New Ideal Man."[1] Whatever *Psychology Today's* reasons for elevating Jesus to that modern pedestal—and despite the fact he had no biological children himself—I find Jesus a perfect role model of the ideal father.

A Christian worldview puts its own spin on how a father understands and practices each of the five habits.

Grasping Your Significance

If you are a follower of Jesus Christ, you recognize the truth that no person is a biological accident, regardless of the circumstances of his or her conception. Each child's unique features, gifts, and personality bear the imprint of a personal and creative God. That new life, the Bible says, is created in the image of God—which includes a *yearning* for God. The Psalmist reminds me that I was known by God even in my mother's womb and that nothing about me is by chance (Psalm 139:13–16).

Therefore both I and my children are significant—and no person or circumstance can take that away.

Neither is any child (including adult children) fatherless or without a fathering model, even if his or her biological father is gone. This is evidence of God's sensitivity to the fact that life isn't perfect; yet he will be there for a child when an earthly father is not.

By divine design you are and always will be significant to your children, whether you are actively present in their lives or not. This explains the fathering power you innately possess. You can use it positively or negatively, but you cannot turn it off.

The Impact of Your Father

No matter what kind of dad you had, your worldview will deeply color the place he holds in your thinking. If you didn't know the man, even that absence made an imprint just as if he had been there during your developing years. If your father's relationship with you (or lack of one) was disappointing or even painful, you have recourse in God, your heavenly Father, to acquire a perfect substitute and a healthy fathering model.

There is also God's spiritual power to heal and put behind you the dull ache or vivid anguish you still may feel because of your father. In God your Father is the hope that you can yet understand and forgive your dad. Whatever his failings or sins against you, he was overwhelmed by the same human condition you and I face in ourselves each day—selfishness and self-centered thinking.

A word about sin: In biblical terms sin is not a laundry list of unapproved behaviors—a cosmic Dirty Dozen or Negative Nine—but an attitude of ignoring God, either passively or actively. I have observed in each of my children an instinct to sin from the earliest days of their lives, in spite of Leslie's and my enormous efforts to make our home a positive and wholesome place to grow. This bent to ignore God is darkly instinctive within each person.

If your belief system does not account for the negative, troubling, unfair, and dark aspects of life, sooner or later you will be visited by confusion and emptiness when your worldview cannot explain or help you face a devastating life situation—a violent act against you or a loved one, a death in the family, a crippling or terminal disease, an unfair or humiliating defeat. What will you do then? What will you say to your children to prepare them for such eventualities? They need to hear it from you.

The biblical worldview squarely addresses the evil that even well-intended people do to one another—including my shortcomings as a dad—and offers a realistic, personal healing.

Acting Intentionally

"It's not hard to make decisions when you know what your values are," asserted Roy Disney (yes, Walt's brother).[2] The trouble is that we are fathering in a culture plagued with fuzzy thinking about bedrock values—especially the question of just how responsible individuals are for their choices and actions. We are all too ready to excuse personal responsibility or else find a scapegoat for it.

Smart Idea:
Discipline yourself to write to your out-of-the-nest children every week. It may be only a cartoon clipping, a two-sentence greeting, or a "What's up with you?" question—but the frequency will keep your relationship growing.

In the car the other day, I caught a news clip on the radio. The city had apparently announced a get-tough approach to its graffiti problems. In the sound bite, a city official explained that they would begin charging parents of "taggers" for the costs of repairing their kids' damage. "It will no longer be acceptable for a parent to argue, 'I just can't control my child,'" the official said.

When did it become tolerable for a father to default on his civic responsibilities to his children—not to mention his emotional and spiritual responsibilities? Where is his intentional action toward the training of his children?

The worldview called Christianity encompasses intentional action somewhat ambiguously. On one hand, Jesus requires a father (as he requires all people) to follow him—to act intentionally "toward" him, so to speak. Yet he makes it equally clear that Christianity is *not* subscribing to a code of conduct, not even a biblical code. This is because to genuinely, consistently follow most codes is beyond any human. The Ten Commandments, Christ's Sermon on the Mount—the worldview advocated by God in such edicts is accurate but unattainable.

Hope lies in one of the meanings of *Christian*—"Christ in one." That is, only by Christ living in me am I able to acquire the spiritual dynamic to father my children as Jesus Christ fathers me. Jesus Christ lives spiritually in me, changing my desires to ones more compatible with effective fathering, empowering me to make tough fathering choices. Faith applied like this, within a Christian worldview, becomes a supra-factor to positive and practical fathering.

Using Your Network

Although I value and celebrate the talents and personality that God gave me, I still don't possess what I need to get through life. I love the clear, haunting tones of a well-played French horn, but that sound does not thrill me like a full brass ensemble. It is realistic, not pessimistic, to admit that I don't have all the answers and gifts and talents that my children need. A Christian worldview assures me of this reality, as well as of the absolute need of the support and balance I receive from others. Worldviews that place me at the center of the universe instead of in the center of friends—that is, dependent—do not easily sustain realistic fathering.

"Be kind and compassionate to one another, forgiving each other, just as in Christ God forgave you," wrote the apostle Paul (Eph. 4:32) in an ancient endorsement of modern networking. When I am as dependent on others as they are on me, I can let my hair down. I don't have to always be right. I can admit that, as a mature and reasonably savvy dad, I still don't know what to do in a given situation. I can admit to other dads my failures and struggles without losing face. And in return I can receive their genuine support and encouragement.

That is networking.

A biblical worldview also helps me select and support other adults who help my child grow up—teachers, neighbors, coaches, bosses. A biblical worldview deepens my appreciation for them and gives me objective criteria for reviewing and evaluating their input.

Communicating Life Skills and Principles

A biblical worldview, of course, offers the wisdom of the Bible as a prime sourcebook for living—a proven, full, and integrated set of life principles, with hundreds of stories that illustrate and exemplify those skills and principles for myself and for my children.

Take the Old Testament book of Daniel, for instance. After a three-month siege late in the seventh century B.C., Jerusalem surrendered to Nebuchadnezzar, who marched many Jewish captives off to Babylon—including a young aristocrat named Daniel. The dilemmas of this nobleman and his companions in the king's court are timeless stories of peer pressure, resisting temptation, and salvation from whatever lions happen to be stalking you at the moment.

Some of God's clearest instruction about what principles a father should teach his children are in Deuteronomy.

> These commandments that I give you today are to be upon your hearts. Impress them on your children. Talk about them when you sit at home and when you walk along the road, when you lie down and when you get up. Tie them as symbols on your hands and bind them on your foreheads. Write them on the doorframes of your houses and on your gates. (Deut. 6:6-9)

Tell your children about how life works. Our society is drifting into destructive ways of interacting because too many fathers are either silent or telling their children the wrong message.

In the previous chapter I told you about the discovery that, despite all my supposedly good parenting, my son Jon became involved with marijuana and substance

Smart Idea:

Encourage a habit of critical thinking and activism in your kids by keeping postcards or stationery and a supply of stamps by your TV. When a program, newscast segment, or political report pleases or annoys you, express your sentiments in writing.

abuse. There are no ironclad guarantees in fathering, I found out. It was the low point so far in my experience as a dad. What had become of all those values, skills, and principles I tried to instill in Jon?

Once the abuse was discovered and we confronted Jon, it took a couple years before we felt somewhat certain that the battle with substance abuse was a winnable war. Prayer to a personal and powerful God was a mainstay during this time. Ultimately, it was our capacity for deeply loving Jon (when his actions were so terribly offensive and unlovable) and God's gentle pursuit of his heart through a variety of circumstances that turned things around.

Once the immediate crisis passed, there began the long process of restoration in the relationship . . . of desiring to see Jon experience real freedom from this season of his youth . . . of desiring to see the life values we thought we had taught all those years be expressed in his daily choices and personal confidence.

I had to bite my tongue sometimes so I wouldn't say what would probably distance us again. At other times, I found myself scrambling for something wise to say as I confronted Jon with my expectations and disappointment about what he was doing.

The phone rang one day, and Leslie recognized the voice as one of Jon's friends who had encouraged his drug abuse. We had prayed that God would either help or remove this friend from Jon's life. In a brief conversation with Leslie, the boy mentioned that *he* was praying about something. Through the influence of a girl he was dating, he had apparently experienced a very real personal encounter with Jesus Christ himself. It had changed his life, and now he was calling Jon out of concern for his old buddy.

In a month of Sundays I wouldn't have guessed that God would choose to work through this friend to tug Jon back to faith. But that's what happened. Jon spent the next weekend with this friend and his girlfriend—attending church with them, learning about the reality of spiritual faith in their lives. It was an important marker in Jon's return to wholeness.

Today Jon is the delight of my heart. He has just about completed his three-year certification as a locksmith and has returned to school to finish college. He's living on his own; we usually meet on Wednesday mornings before work for breakfast. Jon and I both look forward to those times of conversation—sometimes lighthearted, sometimes very serious—but always engaging. I see in his life and conversation, his spiritual interests, the way he treats his girlfriend, and in his desire to help people all the major values Leslie and I had tried to teach and model over the years.

I still believe there are no guarantees. Yet the probability of a happy ending, should you find yourself off-roading as a dad, is vastly improved if the supra-factor or spiritual faith is guiding both your choice of life skills and principles and your ability to live them in front of your kids.

Maximizing Your Moments

You may have heard about the father's trip to the supermarket with his four-year-old son. They found themselves waiting in line at the register, packed into the narrow checkout aisle immediately behind a man who was plainly obese. The youngster took one look at the girth looming over him and said, too loudly, "Hey, Dad, that man is really fat!"

Thoroughly embarrassed but recognizing a teachable moment when it was thrust upon him, the father bent over and told the boy, in one of those intense parental whispers, "We don't talk about people that way! He may be large, but we must be kind in how we talk about him."

The boy missed the point completely. "But, Dad, he really *is* fat!"

The corpulent customer, annoyed now, attempted to turn around in the narrow aisle and see who was raising such a racket. In the process he bumped against the youngster. At the same moment his pager started beeping.

"Look out, Dad!" the kid shouted. "He's backing up!"

Teachable moments, it seems, arrive when you least want them, they're too public for your comfort, and they lack all appearance of Christian charity.

A biblical worldview urges fathers to detect teachable moments wherever and whenever. Without in any way diminishing the freedom of personal choice, a Christian worldview contends that God knows and cares about every detail of every life. God numbers the hairs on my head, Jesus taught, and a sparrow cannot fall to the ground without his knowing. That kind of all-knowing and caring God can coach a father to maximize his moments and number his days with his children.

Your High-Stakes Choice

That is my worldview—ordered by God, personified in Jesus, revealed in the Bible. Whether or not you agree with my belief system, of how I perceive that life works,

Smart Thought:
A famous man is one whose children love him. (French proverb)

you sense the priority and importance I attach to choosing carefully one's personal belief system.

One cannot afford to be wrong on this point. You cannot evaluate this question casually, put it off too long, or leave it to chance. The stakes are just too high, for it concerns heaven and the afterlife.

Jesus was not vague or uncertain about heaven. He came to earth from there, he said. We are to pray to our Father who is listening from heaven. Reliable witnesses—some 500 at one time—saw Jesus ascend into heaven following his resurrection. Far from wishful thinking, heaven is a real place for which there is highly defensible evidence.

I would lay odds on heaven if only for this reason: *If* there is a heaven, I don't want my children to miss it. Like any father, I love my children deeply and want for them the best of everything, including the afterlife. I've never forgotten what a friend remarked to me some years ago. "You realize don't you," he said, "that your children are the only earthly possessions you can take to heaven with you?"

Jesus clearly taught that when he left this earth he was returning to God the Father in heaven, where he would prepare a place for every one who believes in him. And if my children whom I love so much are going to be in heaven for all eternity, I want to be there with them, too. Compared to this, I don't care about my questions and doubts about other Christian teachings. I just wouldn't want to miss an eternity with my kids—and I don't think they want to miss it with me.

Wherever you are or whatever your circumstance at this moment, God wants you and your family to spend eternity with him in heaven; the box office to heaven is always open and your ticket has already been purchased for you by Jesus Christ. All that remains is for you to decide you want to go there and to step up in a simple prayer of gratitude and receive from Jesus Christ his forgiveness for your sins and your paid admission to heaven.

God listens and responds to the prayers of his children, the Bible teaches. Prayer is a secret weapon for a father, a powerful tool for protecting them fully and providing what they need most.

The Power of Praying for Your Children

Look at what a father's prayers accomplish:
• **Prayer keeps me dependent upon God.** Fatherhood can be baffling. Was I too strict or too easy? Were my words loving

enough? Will they forgive me for my temper? Will I someday regret how much time I now give to my job?

Prayer guarantees that I am seeing my fathering role for what it really is—a spiritual calling—and confirms that I'm seeking God's power and the wisdom in the Scriptures to overcome my weaknesses.

• **Prayer sets the stage for successful living.** In instructing followers of Christ to "pray continually" (1 Thess. 5:17), the apostle Paul was saying that prayer ought to create a backdrop for everyday living. Whether it is a misunderstanding with my wife or children or a simmering dispute with a colleague at the office, prayer changes a fractured relationship into a spiritual project.

• **Prayer protects my children.** I'm not in my daughter's classroom to counter a false value served up by a favorite teacher. I can't be there on the playground to contradict a painful, excruciatingly timed remark directed to my child. I can't monitor the billboards, magazines, or commercials that tug at my son's sexual desires.

I really have no option but to ask God to guard my children's minds and emotions from being captured by the evil forces in the world. I must pray, as Paul did for his followers (whom he cared for, he wrote, as a father cares for his children), that they "may be able to discern what is best and may be pure and blameless until the day of Christ" (Phil. 1:10). This is a battle I cannot afford to lose by default.

• **Prayer provides for my children.** At the top of my list of things I want provided for my children, way ahead of the others, is the gift of a spouse they will live happily with for a lifetime. Beside finding their own personal faith in Jesus Christ, I can't think of a more important gift in this lifetime. Ironically, it's a choice I will watch them make when they are probably young and inexperienced.

Yet miracles of a sort can even happen here. Sam was a teenager in southern Oregon when someone presented the story of Jesus Christ to him, and he made a personal spiritual commitment. His spiritual growth took off with a bang and stayed strong. Someone got him his own Bible (with *Sam* stamped on the front cover), which he read voraciously, underlining portions that connected with him, writing notes in the margins.

So it was a particularly dismal day when he lost his Bible somewhere along a

> **Smart Idea:**
> Challenge your family to take a vacation from complaining. Dare them to go twenty-four hours without a complaint. It's not as easy as it sounds; you'll all discover how easily complaining becomes a habit.

trail during a summer backpacking trip. When he got home, he bought another Bible and forgot about the loss.

Four years later Sam was attending college in Southern California and seriously dating the daughter of a Christian family. The weekend her family moved to a new house across town, Sam helped. He was carrying an overfilled book box out the door to the trailer when a book tumbled out of the box onto the sidewalk. Sam set the box down and reached for the book—and in disbelief recognized it as his long-lost Bible.

"Where did you get this Bible?" he asked the family. During a family vacation to southern Oregon a few years earlier, they found it on the trail during a hike. The girl's parents searched for an address so they could mail the Bible to its owner, but all the I.D. they found on it was the imprinted *Sam* on the cover. The more they flipped through it, though, and read through the handwritten notes in the margins, the more they were impressed with the spiritual insight of this "Sam." If only a man with this kind of spiritual heart would marry their daughter, they thought. So they had begun praying, "Please send a man, God, to marry our daughter—a man who loves you as much as 'Sam.'"

In one way or another, your prayers will provide what your children need.

Let's Stay in Touch

The five habits of smart dads aren't clever. Yet I have found in the courses I teach at Dads University—and through conversations with many, many fathers—that this model helps fathers understand their role and stay on track as they leave a positive imprint on their children, a legacy of fatherly love.

My hope is that you will adopt the five key habits of smart dads for yourself. I hope that your fathering is satisfying for both you and your children.

If these five key habits of smart dads help get your fathering on the right road, please write and tell me:

Paul Lewis
Family University
P.O. Box 500050
San Diego, CA 92150-0050.

Notes

Chapter 1

1. Ellen Goodman, "Life without Father: Lost and Found," *The Boston Globe*, April 10, 1992.

2. Henry Biller and Dennis Meredith, *Father Power* (Garden City, New York: Anchor Press/Doubleday, 1975).

3. *The Role of Fathers in America: Attitudes and Behavior*, a Gallup national random sample conducted for the National Center for Fathering, April 14–17, 1992.

4. Nancy R. Gibbs, "Bringing Up Father," *Time* (June 28, 1993), 55.

5. Nina J. Easton, "Life without Father," *Los Angeles Times Magazine* (June 14, 1992), 15.

6. Gibbs, "Bringing Up Father," 55.

7. Alvin Toffler, *The Third Wave* (New York: William Morrow & Co., 1980), 139.

8. Gibbs, "Bringing Up Father," 54.

9. Easton, "Life without Father," 16.

10. Myron Magnet, "The American Family, 1992," *Fortune* (August 10, 1992), 45.

11. Magnet, "The American Family, 1992," 42–47.

12. Easton, "Life without Father," 18.

13. Gibbs, "Bringing Up Father," 54.

14. Magnet, "The American Family, 1992," 46.

15. Ibid.

16. This collection of statistics is found in Barbara Dafoe Whitehead, "Dan Quayle Was Right" (*Atlantic Monthly*, April 1993); Magnet, "The American Family, 1992"; and Gibbs, "Bringing Up Father."

17. Gibbs, "Bringing Up Father," 58.

18. Asa Baber, "The Decade of the Dad," *Playboy* (January 1990), 33.

Chapter 4

1. *The Role of Fathers in America: Attitudes and Behavior,* a Gallup national random sample conducted for the National Center for Fathering, April 14 –17, 1992.

2. Dotson Rader, "'I Want to Be like My Dad'" (interview with Kevin Costner), *Parade Magazine* (January 20, 1991), 5.

3. *The Role of Fathers in America: Attitudes and Behavior.*

4. Sam Osherson, *Finding Our Fathers* (New York: Macmillan, 1986).

5. Easton, "Life without Father," 19. The parenting program is conducted by New York's nonprofit Manpower Demonstration Research Corporation.

Chapter 5

1. Everett Kline, on growing up. Kline's essay is part of *Men's Stories, Men's Lives,* a collection of reminiscences gathered from the National SEED (Seeking Educational Equity and Diversity) Project's first Multicultural Men's Studies Seminar, October 30, 1991.

2. From a 1990 National Center for Fathering news release.

3. Easton, "Life without Father," 16.

4. Shasta L. Mead and George A. Rekers, "Role of the Father in Normal Psychosexual Development," *Psychological Reports,* 45 (1979), 923–24.

5. Mead and Rekers, "Role of the Father," 924, 926.

6. Mead and Rekers, "Role of the Father," 923, 927.

7. Alston & Nanette, 1982; Bach, 1946; Biller, 1976; Biller & Baum, 1971; Carlsmith, 1964; Covell & Turnbull, 1982; Daum & Bieliauskas, 1983; Drake & Mc Dugall, 1977; Fry, 1983; Gershansky, et. al., 1980; Goldstein, 1982, 1983; Hetherington & Deur, 1971; Lynn, 1974, 1976; Matther, 1976; McCord, McCord & Thurber, 1962; Mead & Rekers, 1979; Nask, 1965; Micoli, 1985; Parish & Taylor, 1979; Reis & Gold, 1977; Rekers, 1981, 1986; Shill, 1981; Stoklosa, 1981; Stolz, 1954. All appeared as cites in testimony given on June 12, 1986, Capitol Hill hearing on "The National Family Strengths Project." Testimony given by George A. Reekers, Ph.D., and available from U.S. House of Representatives, Rayburn Office Building Room 2325, Washington, D.C.

8. Whitehead, "Dan Quayle Was Right," 47.

9. Alston & Nannette, 1982; Covell & Turnbull, 1982; Gispert, et al., 1984; Lancaster & Richmond, 1983; Parish & Nunn, 1983; Pomano & Micanti, 1983; Lewis, Newson & Newson, 1982; Hoffman, 1981; Park, 1981; Russell, 1983. See note seven, above.

10. Easton, "Life without Father," 16.

11. Gibbs, "Bringing Up Father," 61.

12. Ibid.

13. Ibid.

14. Ibid.

15. Magnet, "The American Family, 1992," 43.

16. Whitehead, "Dan Quayle Was Right," 47.

17. Qualitative research from a stratified study of 2,066 religious fathers surveyed between October 1988 and February 1990. Comments were compiled from a random sampling of that group.

18. Stephen Covey, *The Seven Habits of Highly Effective People* (New York: Simon and Schuster, 1989), 42–43.

19. Qualitative research of 2,066 religious fathers.

20. Sam Keen and Ofer Zur, "A *Psychology Today* Survey Report: Who Is the New Ideal Man?" *Psychology Today* (November 1989), 54.

21. Rader, "'I Want to Be like My Dad,'" 4.

22. Paul Lewis, *Famous Fathers* (Elgin, Ill.: David C. Cook, 1984), 112.

Chapter 6

1. Qualitative research of 2,066 religious fathers.

2. Ibid.

3. *The Role of Fathers in America: Attitudes and Behavior.*

NOTES

4. Barna Research Group, commissioned by Josh McDowell Ministry in preparation for the Why Wait? Campaign. The study regarded the sexual attitudes and behavior, personal interests and lifestyle, relationship with parents, spiritual beliefs, and demographic traits of 1,483 youths, ages twelve to seventeen.

Chapter 7
1. Covey, *Seven Habits*, 50.
2. Qualitative research of 2,066 religious fathers.
3. Covey, *Seven Habits*, 49.
4. Tom Black, my associate at Family University, is a specialist at helping parents understand motivational patterns and the personal style of their children. His recently published book *Born to Fly!* (Grand Rapids: Zondervan, 1994) is an excellent guide to discerning the strengths, drives, and patterns in yourself as well as in your children.

Chapter 8
1. Gary Smalley and John Trent, *The Blessing* (Nashville: Nelson, 1986).
2. Rader, "'I Want to Be like My Dad,'" 7.

Chapter 9
1. Joe Russo. This writing is part of *Men's Stories, Men's Lives*, a collection of reminiscences gathered from the National SEED (Seeking Educational Equity and Diversity) Project's first Multicultural Men's Studies Seminar, October 1991–May 1992.

Chapter 10
1. Cited in Gibbs, "Bringing Up Father," 58.
2. Gibbs, "Bringing Up Father," 61.

Chapter 11
1. From a brochure from Grand Auto Supply & Tire Service, SKU #890243, November 1991.

Chapter 12
1. Keen and Zur, "The New Ideal Man," 57.
2. Roy Disney is cited by H. Jackson Brown, Jr., in *A Father's Book of Wisdom* (Nashville: Rutledge Hill Press, 1990), 131.

Discussion Guide

CHAPTER 1: Dad, Pop, My Ol' Man, Sir
THEME: *On Being a Father*

Remember Nancy Kingery Myatt's reaction to her father, now suffering from Alzheimer's disease and from whom she'd been separated for twenty-eight years? By merely being your children's father, you have tremendous power in their lives.

- When have you realized the power you have in your children's lives merely because you're their father? Give a specific moment. Name one specific behavior that shows your choice to use that power for your children's good.

- What word picture would you use to illustrate your feelings about fathering? Which word picture (page 16) best describes your feelings about fathering? Explain why you chose that one.

- In what ways do you feel forced to choose between career advancement and deepening relationships with your children? Where do you find guidance and support for your commitment to being a father?

- The section of the chapter beginning with "The Transformation of Fathering" and going through "If Patriarchy Is Passé, Who Am I as a Father?" offers a historical overview of the role of father as well as an evaluation of our culture's perspective on fathering. What is one new insight you gained from this section? What feelings did this historical background and analysis of modern society leave you with? What new (or renewed) conviction about the importance of your fathering—what fire in your belly—did this reading ignite?

- As one dictionary definition of the word "father" suggests, children acquire their sense of significance largely from how their fathers respond to them. What did your father teach you about your worth—and how did he do that? What do you do to show your children that they are significant to you? Be specific. What skills and knowledge do you remember learning from your father? What skills and knowledge have your children learned from you? What new skill would you like to start teaching each of your children?

- **Smart Move:** Choose one of this chapter's "Smart Ideas"—and do it today!

CHAPTER 2: Cruise Control
THEME: *The Power of Your Habits*

Habits are like cruise control: When properly set for the driving conditions, habits add ease and pleasure to the trip. Making the five fathering habits featured in this book part of your life will shape a legacy worth passing on to your children and grandchildren.

- What habits characterized your father's daily routines and behavior? What habits of his fathering do you remember? What habits characterize your day-to-day routine? What destructive fathering habits are you aware of having settled into?

- *Desire* lies at the heart of habit. Each of your habits, good and bad, satisfies some desire. What desires do you have for your fathering? What habitual fathering behaviors support or erode those desires? Which of your habitual fathering habits would you like to replace with more helpful habits? (Keep reading! Ideas to come in the next several chapters!)

- *Direction* serves as the how-to guide we use whenever we choose to do or not do something. To identify the direction in which your fathering is headed, consider what your worldview says about fathering. Do you see fathering as a sprint or a marathon? How has this worldview affected your interaction with your children? Give two or three specific examples. Do you see fathering as the work of an architect or a farmer? How has this perspective affected your interaction with your children? Again, give two or three specific examples.

- *Diligence* is the commitment to repeat the required thought or action continually until it becomes a habit. When have you had the diligence to develop a new habit in your life? What benefits are you reaping from that effort?

- Your *destination* as a father is the legacy you leave for your children after your lifetime. What are some of the features of the legacy you want to leave for your children? What are some good fathering habits that will foster this legacy? (Don't worry if you're unsure at this point! That's what this book is all about!)

- **Smart Move**: Choose one of this chapter's two "Smart Ideas" or its "Smart Thought"—and act today!

CHAPTER 3: The Five Key Habits
THEME: *A Fathering Model*

With an ordinary automobile wheel as the model, I can explain five foundational fathering habits that will help you visualize your role so that you can move beyond where you are to where you want to go— which, of course, is what the wheels on a car help you do.

- Who has served as a model of fathering for you? What have you copied from these men? What behaviors have you intentionally avoided?

- In your estimation, what makes a father successful? List as many specific factors as possible. Circle those factors that are already clearly evident in your fathering.

- What was your initial reaction to the paradigm of fathering illustrated on page 41? Were you encouraged? Discouraged? Overwhelmed? Helped? Interested in reading more? Explain.

- Review the descriptions of the elements of the "fathering wheel"—the axle, lug nuts, rim, tire, and tread (pages 41–43). Which element of your fathering wheel do you think is the weakest? (Have no fear! There's hope! The chapter which focuses on that part of the wheel will be a great help to you!)

- Which element of your fathering wheel do you feel is the strongest? (Good! That's a foundational point on which to build as you read about that part of the wheel as well as the other four!)

- **Smart Move**: Choose one of the chapter's "Smart Ideas"—and do it today!

CHAPTER 4: Dad in the Rearview Mirror
THEME: *Your Father's Imprint on Your Life*

Recognizing and dealing with your father's imprint on you is a prerequisite to acquiring the five key habits of smart dads. By accentuating the positive and processing the negative in your father's relationship with you, you unleash a power and freedom for shaping your own fathering style.

- What word best describes the most prominent feature of your relationship with your father? Was your father's relationship with you mostly good or mostly bad, or are you neutral about it?

- A father's influence reaches far beyond his own children, but consider for a moment just how significant your father's influence is on you, the first generation after him. First, how do your abilities and appearance reflect your father's genetic influence on you? Second, what patterns for relating to other people have their roots in your relationship and interaction with your family members, including your father? Third, when have you responded or, in an emotionally charged moment, reacted to your children in a way that your father reacted to you? Finally, complete the "Family Genogram" (page 51) as a way of identifying any unhealthy ways of relating that have repeated themselves for one or more generations in your family.

- Now, if you haven't already, get out your pencil and answer the "Seven Quick Questions" found on page 52; focus especially on questions 5 and 6. What unresolved issues with your father—if any (and most of us have them)—do your answers suggest?

- Resolving a poor childhood relationship with your father calls for you to recognize the problem, see your father in a new light, presume your father craved the love and respect of his children, and give your father what he will not or cannot ask for—forgiveness. If you need to resolve your relationship with your father, which step are you at? Whom will you ask to encourage you, pray for you, and hold you accountable as you take the next step toward forgiving your father? What will that next step be—and when will you take it?

- What was the most significant thing your father ever did with you? How would you like your children to answer that question? Also, what epitaph would you like your children to inscribe on your tombstone? The next five chapters will give you practical ideas for living up to the epitaph you just drafted!

- **Smart Move:** Choose one of the chapter's "Smart Ideas" or "Smart Tips"—and do it today!

CHAPTER 5: Habit One: Grasping Your Significance
THEME: *The Axle*

Just as a car axle is the point of contact between the wheel assembly and the rest of the car, comprehending your significance as a father is what connects your fathering to the rest of your life.

- What about how you use your time and how you've established your priorities reflects your understanding of your significance as a father? Give four or five specific examples—or consider what action you might take if examples are sparse.

- Let the sections entitled "A Positive and Continuous Relationship," "A Father Brings a Unique Strength," and "More Than Substitute Mothers" (pages 68–70) serve as a mirror for you and evaluate how you're doing on the following counts. For each item, tell of a behavior, a statement, or an interaction with a child that reflects your strength in that category. At the same time, however, determine what you could be doing to be stronger in that category. Be specific.

  — Being a positive presence in the home (in contrast to merely being there)

  — Focusing on the quality of the father-child relationship (as opposed to frequency of interactions)

  — Being a leader in the home (dominant but not domineering)

  — Enforcing socially acceptable standards

  — Fostering "socially viable children"

  — Encouraging children to face and conquer challenges

  — Nurturing your marriage and thereby providing children with a sense of security and safety *or* mitigating the downside of a divorce that has already happened

- What are the two biggest barriers you face in wanting to be a good dad? Realize that—whatever your limitations—your availability to and love for your children are central to their well-being. You are significant to your child exactly as you are this moment. Despite that fact, what specific steps will you take to overcome those barriers you just identified and to change yourself on the inside so you'll be a better father on the outside?

- In your mind, what makes a father successful? As you reach for those goals, start by giving your children your love, your approval, and your encouragement. What specific act of love (make your child feel important to you!), approval (offer honest praise, not generic or exaggerated compliments), and encouragement (cheer your child on!) will you give each of your children today?

- What fact, result of research, or simple statement in this chapter has most helped you realize your significance as a father?

Whom do you know who grasps his significance as a father? What characteristic of his fathering example would you do well to imitate?

- **Smart Move:** Choose one of the chapter's "Smart Ideas" or "Smart Tips"—and do it today!

CHAPTER 6: Habit Two: Acting Intentionally
THEME: *The Lug Nuts*

Lug nuts secure the wheel to the axle. In fathering, your intentional actions (lug nuts) connect your understanding of your significance as a father (axle) to the living out of that understanding in your relationship with your children (the rim, tire, etc.). So let's tighten those lug nuts!

- **Lug Nut 1: Be proactive—accept full responsibility for your fathering role.** Copy down the list of ideas for five-minute fathering (pages 85–86). Which suggestion will you follow today in order to manage your life and resources in a way that displays your love for your children?

- **Lug Nut 2: Set clear, measurable goals for fathering.** What are the three most important long-range and three most important short-range goals you have for your relationship with your children? Write these desires down and then turn them into measurable goals and manageable steps (grab a calendar!). Think in terms of personal goals about what you want to teach your children, family vacations you want to take before they leave home, etc. Also, over pizza one night, ask family members—one at a time—to list what they want to accomplish in the next twelve months and discuss how the whole family can help each person reach his or her goals. (See specific suggestions for setting goals on page 90, tools on pages 92 and 94, and samples on pages 93 and 95.)

- **Lug Nut 3: Make and keep commitments that help you fulfill fathering goals.** If you haven't already, use the form on page 96 to inventory how you use your time. Then cut your commitments if you have to in order to make one-on-one, focused fathering time for each of your children. Schedule those times as you would a business appointment. Also target and schedule opportunities to say or demonstrate your love for your kids.

- **Lug Nut 4: Regularly review and evaluate your progress toward fathering goals.** Reviewing goals and evaluating our progress toward them keeps us moving—and moving in the right direction. So grab your calendar and schedule four hours sometime about ninety days from now to evaluate the goals you set when you tightened Lug Nut 2.

- **Lug Nut 5: Correct your course as necessary to reach fathering goals.** Whenever you preview and review your fathering week—and especially when you review your progress after ninety days—correct your course as necessary. In the shorter term, what course corrections in your fathering did the events of today suggest to you? Be specific—and then adjust your sails!

- **Smart Move:** Choose one of the chapter's "Smart Ideas" or "Smart Tips"—and do it today!

CHAPTER 7: Habit Three: Using Your Network
THEME: *The Rim*

A network is as necessary to your fathering as a strong rim is to your wheel's performance. Three relationships intersect to form your primary fathering network—your personality, style, and talents; your child's personality, styles, talents, and development; and the child's mother's input and support.

- **Your personality, style, and talents**. What personal management style are you carrying over into your fathering style? For instance, are you a hands-on manager or a delegator? A naturally strong leader or a naturally strong background/support person? Next, what inborn talents and natural abilities do you bring to your fathering? (The historical-intelligence method described on pages 108–9 can help you identify these strengths.) Now match your list of natural abilities to the five key habits of fathering. What do you do naturally that is smart fathering? How can you father so that you're playing to these strengths? Be specific. Finally, who and what will you add to your fathering network (the mother of your child, other fathers, outside resources) to compensate for those areas where you aren't naturally gifted?

- **Your child's personality, style, talents, and development**. As a student of your children, what is one thing you've learned about each of them in the last two weeks? Now list five style and character qualities that make each of your children unique. Next, have you photocopied a developmental chart or two? (If not, do so now!) What did the charts help you understand about your child and how has this understanding improved your fathering? Finally, what learning style (visual, auditory, hands-on) does each of your children prefer? How have you or will you adapt your fathering based on this insight?

- **The child's mother.** The mother can often read a child's emotional condition more readily or be more aware of what is typical behavior than a father can. When have you seen this to be true? Give a specific example or two. What regular time have you set apart to get insight from your children's mother about their personality, style, and talents? What did you learn from her in your most recent conversation? What did you learn about yourself and your fathering when you asked her for her perspective on your personality, style, and abilities? (It's worth the risk of asking!) What are you working on as a result of that discussion? And, finally, what specific encouragement did she have for you? What did she say is one positive aspect of the fathering you're already doing?

- Have you taken a step toward doubling your fathering confidence and cutting your anxiety in half? In other words, have you started to lay the foundation for—or are you already involved in—a small group of other dads who meet to talk about fathering? Look again at the parameters and steps outlined on pages 113–14 and take advantage of the opportunity to receive this kind of support. (If you're a divorced father or are separated from your children's mother, find or develop a support group of fathers in similar circumstances. And once again review the advice on page 112. Take action on any or all of these points if you haven't already.)

- What do you do to monitor the impact teachers, counselors, youth leaders, coaches, and neighbors are making in your children's life? What do you do to encourage these other players in your children's life? How has the input of your children's teacher, coach, employer, or friends helped you be a better father? Finally, what book, tape, video, seminar, or class on fathering (some are suggested on pages 116–17) does it sound like you would benefit from? Find out by purchasing, ordering, or enrolling today!

- **Smart Move:** Choose one of the chapter's "Smart Ideas" or "Smart Tips"—and do it today!

CHAPTER 8: Habit Four: Communicating Life Skills and Principles
THEME: *The Tire*

The fourth key habit of smart dads is giving your children a working understanding of the life skills, principles, and fundamentals they will need to function successfully as adults in a world which, in twenty years, will be a very different world from ours today.

- Assume the viewpoint of your father and introduce yourself, his son. Then move into the skills, lessons, and insights your father taught you. What did he give you to help you function successfully as an adult? What is your specific plan for preparing your children to function as adults—thinking for themselves; adopting the values of truth, fairness, love, integrity, and loyalty; accepting responsibility for themselves; loving and obeying God? (If you don't have a game plan at this point, keep going. That's what this chapter is all about!)

- After each of the four techniques to help your children learn how to think (listed below), write out a specific opportunity you will have to use that technique for each of your children—and then use it! Keep following these suggestions until they become healthy fathering habits!

  — Ask questions (*what* questions are better than *why* questions!).

  — Let them choose between good options (define firm limitations, outline clear consequences, and clearly communicate those consequences).

  — Let them tell you why (thinking about rules cultivates active, healthy consciences).

  — Help them find their own answers (which of the teachable opportunities listed in the two bullets at the bottom of page 123 and the two bullets at the top of page 124 can you seize?).

- Some of our basic family rules are listed on pages 122–23. What about the tone and wording of these rules appeals to you? What basic family rules have you established for your home? How clearly are these rules understood by your children? To find out, ask them tonight at dinner! Make a game out of outlining your family rules.

- Review the following list of communication principles, practices, and skills (described on pages 124–34). Rank them in the order in which you need to work on them ("1" being the item you'll focus on this week). What will you do to sharpen the skill you most need to work on? Be specific about your plan and then take action!

— Communicate with a spirit of love—and demonstrate your active love for them.

— Build communication bridges by blessing your child.

— Let your children learn from your experience and your example.

— Demonstrate the skills you want to teach them.

— Release children progressively through life.

— Let young children learn from experience.

— Monitor teenage children with vigilance.

— Discipline.

— Teach children to get along with others.

— Keep communication lines open.

— Celebrate rites of passage.

• Review the list of life skills and principles (page 133) that I want each of my children to know by their junior year in high school. Which of these do you have on your list for your children? What else have you added? You may have added some of the items listed on page 135. What are you doing (you need to be intentional!) to ensure that each of your children is making progress on each of these counts?

• **Smart Move:** Choose one of the chapter's "Smart Ideas"—and do it today!

CHAPTER 9: Habit Five: Maximizing Your Moments
THEME: *The Tread*

In our fathering paradigm, the tread on the tire represents maximizing your moments with your children. Use these moments of relationship and interchange between your child and you—the mundane as well as the magical—to know them, express your love for them, teach and guide them, and let them know you.

• What physical evidence of you have you already set aside for your children? What kinds of pictures, videos, audio recordings, notes, letters, and clippings that reflect your values would you like to compile for each child before they leave home? Be specific. When do you or will you work on this important project? Schedule some time.

- Children spell love "t-i-m-e." What does your personal calendar reflect about the love you're communicating to each of your children? What do the reserves of emotional energy you come home with tell your children about how important they are to you? What specific step will you take this week to find in your schedule some one-on-one time for each of your children? And what will you do to come home with more emotional energy for your children? Whom will you ask to hold you accountable in both of these areas?

- Play enhances a child's self-esteem, builds bridges, and builds respect. What are some of your kids' favorite ways to play with you? Be specific about each child's preferences. When was the last time you played with your children? When will you next play with them?

- Be creative when it comes to maximizing your time with your kids—even when you're away from them. What will you do in response to each of the following suggestions? Identify the particulars for each of your children.

  — Choose the right place. Where does each of your children seem most open to you?

  — Choose the right time. When does each of your children open up to you?

  — Be prepared to use stray moments. Create a moment by acting on one of the ideas listed on page 144.

  — Leave behind Post-It notes. Jot one out for each child—and one for your wife—right now.

  — Read a bedtime story to your toddler over the phone or record it on a cassette tape before you leave. Are your photocopied stories or your tape in the ready position for your next overnighter?

  — Rely on the U.S. mail. Do you have pre-addressed and pre-stamped envelopes and postcards in your briefcase for the next time you travel?

  — Review the "checklist for traveling dads" (pages 145–46). What suggestion will you try the next time you travel? And don't necessarily limit yourself to just one!

— Look again at the "essentials for long-distance dads" (page 146). Which essentials have you let slide? Get back on course today!

- Here are a few more moments with your children that you can maximize:

  — **Your moments of weakness.** What mistake, weakness, failure, or problem have you recently let your children see you deal with? What do you think they learned—or, if you had been more open, could have learned—from your example?

  — **Your child's big moments.** What recital, performance, big game, or school event is coming soon? What will you do to celebrate that moment? And what will you do to make your child's next birthday the event that tells her you're glad beyond words that she is alive?

  — **A "trophy moment."** What recent achievement or upcoming milestone can you celebrate? Have you started your special photo album commemorating your child's achievements?

  — **Moments of crisis.** What provisions have you made so that your child can reach you in a crisis? See the suggestions on page 148.

- **Smart Move:** Choose one of the chapter's "Smart Ideas"—and do it today!

CHAPTER 10: Nicks, Scrapes, and Gouges
THEME: *Taking Your Habits on the Road*

Real-life fathering can be messy. Don't think for a minute that the five key habits of smart dads will make your fathering experience neat and tidy. What they will do, though, is assist you to your destination: a mutually satisfying relationship with your kids and, eventually, a positive imprint on their lives.

- If you haven't already, balance those wheels by taking the self-test on page 151. What do your answers to these seven questions tell you about yourself? What changes do you want to make as a result of what you see here? When will you take the first step—and who will hold you accountable for improving your fathering balance?

- What signs are there on the home front (specifically in your interactions with your children) that your life is out of alignment? What adjustments in your schedule do you need to make to bring your fathering back into alignment with your other roles—husband, employee or owner, son of elderly parents, weekend tennis player, bass fishing enthusiast, soccer coach, community volunteer, civic activist, church leader?

- Look into the mirror offered by the section "No Modifications Necessary." Where, if at all, do you see yourself in that discussion? Which point of advice seems most directed to you and what will you do in response to it?

- If you've been fathering for a while, point out how your fathering has been affected by different seasons of your life. When has it easily taken center stage? When has fathering been on the back burner? What new season are you anticipating? How do you think it will affect your ability to be the father you want to be? What will you do to prevent any negative impact it may have on this most important job? If you're about to start on the adventure of fathering or have a newborn in your home, act on the suggestions found on pages 155–56. Then note how doing so affects your attitude toward fathering and your relationship with your soon-to-be-born or just-born child.

- To get new fathering habits rolling, use the chart on page 159 and list your ideas for putting each of the five key habits of fathering into action (see page 156). If you've already done this, review your list and add any new ideas you have. Now choose one of the simple, workable action steps you listed and do it right now!

- **Smart Move:** Choose one of the chapter's "Smart Ideas"—and do it today!

CHAPTER 11: Burnin' Rubber
THEME: *The Tire Track: Your Fathering Legacy*

Your fathering legacy is the record or imprint of those moments and experiences you share with your child. Each is like a part of the tread pattern of a tire. And just as little imprint is left behind by a bald tire, it's intentional moments of performance that count in fathering, not wonderful intentions.

- It's a dangerous gap we all fall into—that gap between our great plans and our actual performance. Which fathering habits that you've been learning about in this book have you tended to showcase rather than use? Where have you developed good intentions rather than taken positive steps toward better fathering?

- Preventive fathering, like preventive car maintenance, can save you big trouble and great cost later. Take a quick inventory of your driving habits:
  - Is your life overinflated? Are you too busy? What commitments and activities—even good things—do you need to drop in order to be the father you want to be?
  - Are you trying to drive yourself and/or your children too fast? Where are you pushing your children to grow up too soon? Where are you rushing your own growth into the skills, knowledge, and habits of good fathering?
  - What upcoming potholes, obstacles, and curbs are you aware of? What issues will each of your children face in the next stage of their life? What questions will each child ask? How ready are you to answer them? Also, do you know the early warning signs of errant behavior like substance abuse or depression?
  - Do you easily spin your wheels by offering big plans and lots of promises? What intentional actions would better demonstrate your commitment to your wife and your children?
  - Are you open to getting competent professional help if your family were to experience a blowout? Resolve any hesitation now so that, when a crisis arrives, you're ready to take positive, helpful action.
- The fathering journey will take you through all kinds of driving conditions.
  - What kind of off-road driving—dealing with unexpected terrain and unmarked territory—have you already had to do? What resources helped you? What did you learn from that experience?
  - What tends to make you drowsy as you father? Do you need to pull over and get some rest right now? What will give you that vital rest?
  - Which road hazards are you facing? Emotional (or worse) abuse of your wife and kids? Workaholism? Perfectionism? Busyness? What hazards are real for your children? Gang involvement, recreational drug use, alcohol abuse, promiscuous

sex, AIDS, abortion, molestation? What are you doing to help your kids steer clear of these dangers?

— What modern road signs are pointing your children in a direction you don't want them to go? What are you doing about society's flipped warning signs regarding gross materialism, evolution, and safe sex? Be specific about the action you're taking.

• Which myth of fathering are you most susceptible to—big moments count most; strong fathers stand alone; pain is pointless; or great fathering is just around the corner? What are you doing to counteract this false thinking—to invest in small moments; to establish a network of healthy relationships with other fathers; to use your children's difficulties and problems as painful but valuable opportunities for them to learn life skills and values; or to not postpone time with your kids? Be specific about the actions you're taking.

• Which of these four common fathering mistakes do you find yourself making—demanding common ground on your turf; expecting adult behavior and reasoning too early; having a short fuse and explosive anger; or failing to choose your battles wisely? Correct those mistakes!

— What is each of your children interested in? Let that be the turf you meet on!

— Which of your children's tasks can you clarify and which expectations can you more clearly define for them? By a brief Q-and-A session with your child (like mine with Shelley), you can better recognize age-appropriate expectations and then help your children succeed in living up to those expectations.

— What signal could your wife or even your children give you to let you know you're getting angry? And what words will you use to ask forgiveness the next time the anger comes anyway and you hurt your kids? Keep short accounts with your family by admitting when you've blown it and asking their forgiveness.

— What battles center on issues that matter, that are fundamental to the values you want to instill in your children? What battles are really worth fighting? You'll gain a lot more of your children's respect when you defend unflinchingly only those things that truly matter.

• **Smart Move:** Choose one of the chapter's "Smart Ideas" or "Smart Tips"—and do it today!

CHAPTER 12: Authentic Father Power
THEME: *Tapping the Supra-Factor*

Your foundational view of life and your spiritual moorings will enormously impact the way you father. For me, a very personal relationship with God—our heavenly Father—has been key to directing and energizing my efforts to father. A Christian worldview puts its own spin on how a father understands and practices each of the five key habits of a smart dad.

• **Grasping your significance and acknowledging the impact of your father.** What significance does your worldview give you? What does it offer if your father's impact on you was disappointing or painful? What does faith in Jesus Christ offer a believer on these two counts?

• **Acting intentionally.** What bedrock values undergird the way you live—and what is their source? What does your set of values say about personal responsibility? What hope for becoming an effective father and making tough fathering choices does a Christian—a person in whom Christ lives—find in his faith?

• **Using your network.** Does your worldview give you permission to be dependent? Explain. What does a biblical worldview offer a father when it comes to networking?

• **Communicating life skills and principles.** What is the source of the principles you are passing on to your children? Are they tested by time? Are they proven by exemplary people? What hope do these life skills and principles offer you for the off-road experiences of fathering? Even if you're not a believer, explain what my faith in the teachings of the Bible and the sovereignty of God has done for me in my twenty-five years of fathering and specifically during my off-roading times with Jon.

• **Maximizing your moments.** What does your worldview say about the passage of time ... about the force which put this world together ... and about the purpose of life on this earth? What does a Christian worldview, which contends that God knows and cares about every detail of every life, say in answer to those questions? If you're not sure, I invite you to find out. You can start by reading the gospel of Mark. After getting to know Jesus a little better, I invite you to accept—if you haven't already—my earlier invitation to say a simple prayer of gratitude and receive from Jesus Christ his forgiveness for your sins and your paid admission to heaven.

- As we close this study, allow me an extra question—one which addresses prayer, an extremely powerful and effective tool that God makes available to us fathers. As I wrote in the text, prayer keeps me dependent on God and guarantees that I see my fathering as a spiritual calling. Prayer is a healing, sustaining, and nurturing backdrop for daily living and daily parenting. Prayer protects my children, their minds, and their emotions—something impossible for me to do myself. Prayer also provides for my children the things they need, the things I desperately want them to have and have no other way to give them. What keeps you from praying or from praying as fervently and faithfully as you'd like? What will you do to remove those barriers, one at a time? How has God responded to your prayers for your children in the past? What specific concerns are the focus of your current prayers for your kids? Write them down so you can thank the Lord when he answers—because he will!

- **Smart Move:** Choose one of the chapter's "Smart Ideas"—and do it today!

If you've been working through these questions with a small group and have an extra week in your thirteen-week session, have I got a plan for you! For Week #13, do something with all the kids. Ideally, all you dads will get together with all the kids but, depending on your children, smaller groups divided according to their ages and interests might mean more fun will be had by all. If you've been working through these questions on your own, celebrate your efforts—and your renewed efforts at fathering—by celebrating your kids. Go play with them! Enjoy them! Let them know that you treasure them.

The College of Fathering at
Family University is...

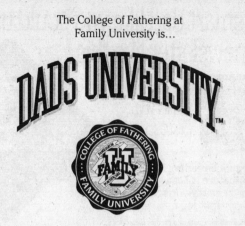

Fathers heading home in the 90s want help!

DADS UNIVERSITY is a "college without walls" program hosted across America by community, corporate, and church organizations concerned with encouraging effective fathering. Featuring a practical curriculum of half-day courses and taught by a national team of certified instructors, the mission of DADS "U" is to help men enjoy their children and raise them successfully—whether toddlers or teenagers.

Courses are a creative mix of lecture, Q&A, video clips, and group interaction. The emphasis is always on ideas for practical application.

Current course offerings include:

Secrets of Fast-Track Fathering
Fathering Confidence: Shaping Your Winning Style
The Seven Secrets of Successful Kids
Discovering Your Child's Design

For more information contact:
The College of Fathering
Family University
P.O. Box 500050
San Diego, CA 92150-0050
Voice: (619) 487-7099 · FAX: (619) 487-7356

A smart dad like you could use a newsletter like this...

Paul Lewis cordially invites you to subscribe!

Every quick-reading *Smart DADS* feature hands a busy father like you the creative ideas, tips, and insights you need to:

- ☑ Turn small moments into lifetime memories
- ☑ Uniquely motivate each of your children
- ☑ Nurture your family's emotional and spiritual health
- ☑ Understand the issues confronting men, children, and families in our society
- ☑ Recognize your child's developmental stages
- ☑ Balance your career and family priorities
- ☑ Build into your children the skills which support maturity and personal achievement
- ☑ Communicate and have everyday fun with toddlers to teenagers
- ☑ Keep your marriage relationship fun, growing, and fulfilling
- ☑ and much more.

PLUS, each "DAD TALK" audio cassette brings you in-depth discussions on such fathering issues as sex education, money, motivation, and the stages of marriage.

....

☐ **YES!** Please enter my subscription to *Smart DADS* newsletter. I understand that a "Dad Talk" cassette will arrive with each third, bi-monthly issue and that, should I become dissatisfied, the unfulfilled portion of my subscription will be cheerfully refunded.

☐ Send me a year of *Smart Dads* (6 issues and 2 tapes) at the special introductory rate of $18.50.
That's 23% off the regular price!

Name _____

Address _____

City/State/Zip _____

Phone: (____) _____

☐ This is a gift subscription. My name and address are attached. Please send a gift card signed:

_____

Payment method (check one):

☐ Check enclosed
☐ Please charge my   ☐ VISA   ☐ MasterCard

No. ☐☐☐☐ — ☐☐☐☐ — ☐☐☐☐ — ☐☐☐☐

Expires _____ Signature: _____

Mail this coupon to:
**SMART DADS
Family University
P.O. Box 500050
San Diego, CA 92150-0050**